The Devil in Dover

The Devil in Dover

An Insider's Story of Dogma v. Darwin
in Small-Town America

LAURI LEBO

THE NEW PRESS

NEW YORK
LONDON

Requests for permission to reproduce selections from this book should be mailed to:
Permissions Department, The New Press, 38 Greene Street, New York, NY 10013.

Published in the United States by The New Press, New York, 2008
Distributed by W. W. Norton & Company, Inc., New York

LIBRARY OF CONGRESS CATALOGING-IN-PUBLICATION DATA
Lebo, Lauri.
The devil in Dover : an insider's story of dogma v. Darwin
in small-town america / Lauri Lebo.
p.   cm.
Includes bibliographical references and index.
ISBN 978-1-59558-208-9
1. Kitzmiller, Tammy—Trials, litigation, etc. 2. Dover Area School District
(Dover, Pa.)—Trials, litigation, etc. 3. Trials—Pennsylvania—Dover.
4. Evolution (Biology)—Study and teaching (Secondary)—Law and legislation—
Pennsylvania—Dover (Township) 5. Intelligent design (Teleology)—Study and
teaching (Secondary)—Law and legislation—Pennsylvania—Dover (Township)
I. Title.
KF228.K589L43 2008
345.73'0288—dc22   2007045959

The New Press was established in 1990 as a not-for-profit alternative to the large,
commercial publishing houses currently dominating the book publishing industry.
The New Press operates in the public interest rather than for private gain, and is
committed to publishing, in innovative ways, works of educational, cultural, and
community value that are often deemed insufficiently profitable.

www.thenewpress.com

Composition by The INFLUX House
This book was set in Bembo.
Printed in the United States of America

2 4 6 8 10 9 7 5 3 1

Dedicated to the Danbury Baptists, Thomas Jefferson,
and to the Separation of Church and State

A few weeks before the Kitzmiller v. Dover Area School District trial began, Bruce Springsteen introduced "Part Man, Part Monkey," at a concert in Newark, New Jersey by saying "Dover, PA—they're not sure about evolution. Here in New Jersey, we're countin' on it."

Part Man, Part Monkey

They prosecuted some poor sucker in these United States
For teaching that man descended from the apes
They coulda settled that case without a fuss or fight
If they'd seen me chasin' you, sugar, through the jungle last night
They'da called in that jury and a one two three said
Part man, part monkey, definitely

[. . .]

Well did God make man in a breath of holy fire
Or did he crawl on up out of the muck and mire
Well the man on the street believes what the bible tells him so
Well you can ask me, mister, because I know
Tell them soul-suckin' preachers to come on down and see
Part man, part monkey, baby that's me

—Bruce Springsteen

Contents

Prologue   xi

1. You Have Much Skill   1
2. Neighbor Against Neighbor   8
3. Met on the Battlefield   26
4. Myth of Separation   48
5. "Never Said It"   69
6. Kidnapped by Baptists   87
7. A Little Constitutional Violation   108
8. Where Every House Is a Palace   131
9. Forty Days   149
10. Seeking Comfort   177
11. "Breathtaking Inanity"   192
12. The Sheep and the Goats   206

    Acknowledgments   225
    Notes   227
    Index   231

Prologue

When I was in junior high, I developed a crush on a reporter. The father of a friend of mine, he worked in the Harrisburg Bureau of the *Pittsburgh Post-Gazette*. Ed Jensen was paunchy and bald, and he probably drank too much. He played card games of hearts with colleagues in the statehouse newsroom all day and filed his stories just before deadline.

He was funny and smart, and his shelves were filled with books by authors like Nabokov and Dostoevsky—names that sounded exotic to my young ear. Most importantly, Mr. Jensen loved to talk with his daughter's friends, listening intently to our stories about school and sports and dating. I thought he was the coolest guy in the world.

Attracted to the idea of working at a job in which I could sit around and play cards and have oh-so-clever conversations, I decided to be a journalist.

On March 28, 1979, five miles from my home, the nuclear reactor at Three Mile Island overheated. Amid fears of meltdown, thousands of people fled central Pennsylvania. Ed Jensen stayed. It wasn't his beat, but he sent his wife and children home to Pittsburgh, while he remained behind. He filed daily reports because he believed in the importance of his job.

Three years later, he died of cancer and I understood what it means to be a reporter. Every now and then, in between the card games and the legislature press conferences and United Way dinners, journalists get to report on a story that makes a difference.

I have been a reporter for eighteen years. Most of my career has been spent writing and reporting on the community where I was raised. In that time, I've gotten to cover a lot of amazing stories and meet many wonderful people. Even though I've never played cards in the newsroom, it's been an incredibly pleasurable and rewarding job. Sometimes, such as the days spent in the federal courtroom covering Dover's battle, I've marveled that I was getting paid to have so much fun.

For years, I had an old *Washington Post* cartoon taped to my desk. It was a picture of a dartboard under a sign that said, "What am I an expert in?" People were hurling darts at the board, each section of which was labeled with a different topic: politics, local government, air quality, nuclear regulatory issues. The tagline of the cartoon said, "How a journalist starts his day." I've always felt that aptly summed up what a lot of us do.

On any given day, I walked into the office with no idea where I was going to go, or who I was going to get to talk to before the day was over. On spring days, when the redbuds were blooming, I called up my sources and said, "Get me out of the office. Let's go for a ride." I've danced the Virginia reel under the stars, surrounded by men in Civil War uniforms and beautiful women in hoop skirts and lovely coiled hair. I've been kissed by a capuchin monkey wearing a diaper. I've petted a mountain lion. I've hiked Pickett's Charge on a dusty summer afternoon, musing over Faulkner.

I've listened to an elementary school principal tell me what it's like to put herself in between a class of five-year-olds and a man wielding a machete. I watched as she traced the scars of her hands where the machete cut through her fingers and down to her palms and said, "My hands are ugly now." I went back to the newsroom and put together a story in which I wrote, "She's wrong. Her hands are beautiful."

And occasionally, I believed I wrote stories that made a difference.

But that belief was dealt a blow following Dover's trial. I had been invited to speak at "Evolution 2006," a conference hosted by Stony Brook University's Department of Ecology and Evolution. Organizers asked me to speak about my coverage of the Dover trial as part of a symposium that included one of Dover's plaintiffs, the plaintiffs' attorneys, and the trial's science experts.

It was not an unusual invitation. Journalists frequently give speeches to different organizations.

But when my editors learned of the invitation, they told me that I was not permitted to participate. Despite months of coverage in which I wrote of the vacuity of intelligent design, my editors feared I might come across, as one editor said, as "pro-evolution." The conference was the joint annual meeting of the Society for the Study of Evolution (SSE), the Society of Systematic Biologists (SSB), and the American Society of Naturalists (ASN). The newspaper's managing editor, Randy Parker, said in a letter to me that these organizations are "all representing a one-sided interest."

Editors told me that scientists had "a vested interest in the outcome of the national debate" over evolution and intelligent design; therefore, it could be perceived as a conflict of interest and I could jeopardize the newspaper's objectivity. I was told that if I defied the newspaper's directive not to speak there, I would be "subject to discipline, up to and including dismissal."

I was deeply frustrated that an institution that championed the First Amendment would try to silence one of its reporters;

ultimately we entered a standoff that lasted several months. Finally they relented. I was allowed to speak, as long as I agreed not to mention the name of my newspaper in my speech.

Unfortunately, that's the state of journalism today. All too often those entrusted to sift through the facts and tell the truth are urged to merely parrot the statements of others, without addressing the context of the story, and we are taught that journalism is simply airing the two sides to every disagreement. All too often we are afraid to stand up for what we know to be true.

The Devil in Dover

1

You Have Much Skill

Why I've heard people say God cannot be alive . . .
if they'll call on him and just believe
                    —*Loretta Lynn, "God Makes No Mistakes"*

I sit across from my father in a Chinese all-you-can-eat buffet restaurant. It is near closing time, and the room is empty save for a single waiter hovering next to us with a pitcher. I take a sip of water. The man swoops in and tops off my glass. Sip. Pour. Sip. Pour. I wish he'd go away.

The restaurant sits in a strip mall and is decorated in garish combinations of red and gold. The food here is covered in heavy sweet-and-sour sauces to appeal to local Pennsylvania Dutch palates. Mashed potatoes are served alongside General Tso's chicken. "You like this kind of food?" my father asks me. He finds this place exotic. This both infuriates me and breaks my heart.

I am trying to reassure him. My devoutly fundamentalist Christian father is afraid, I can tell, and he chooses his words carefully. He is unable to come right out and ask the question I know weighs most heavily on his mind: Do I, his oldest daughter, believe in God?

However, my father can't ask that question. What if the answer is no? And so, he protects himself, and me, by tiptoeing around the subject, searching for clues in a discussion of evolutionary theory. Do I believe we came from apes? Then how come monkeys still exist? I say a person can believe in both evolution and God. He nods his head patiently. He doesn't believe me.

I gnaw on a cuticle, though I know my father hates this. "Quit biting your nails," he says. I slump in my chair and sigh, behaving like a petulant child, even though I am forty-one years old. As a small-town reporter at the *York Daily Record*, I spend much of my time writing stories about municipal millage rates and fundraisers for little girls fighting leukemia. But for the past six weeks, the national spotlight has been shining on my backyard. From a front-row seat in a federal courtroom, I watched elected officials of a school board in nearby Dover, Pennsylvania, try to force religion into science class through a backdoor called intelligent design.

In October 2004, seventeen years after the U. S. Supreme Court struck down the teaching of creation science, Dover's tiny school district adopted its bastard son.

It marked the first time American public school students had been required to learn about intelligent design, the concept that life's complexity demands a guiding hand. Publicly, Dover's school board members spoke of their commitment to sound science education, but privately, behind closed doors, they spoke of leading this nation in a Christian revolution.

And along the way, they bore false witness, and they slandered others.

My father, like many in Dover and across the country, believes that those who oppose the school board are leading an attack on Christian values. In his mind, this was just another ACLU-backed attempt to destroy God.

But what Dean Lebo, my father, refuses to believe, and what I have been unable to make him understand, is that what played out here in our community was faith based on deception. This isn't a story about God versus science, but one of truth versus lies.

The evidence is overwhelming. The mechanics of evolutionary theory—natural selection and genetic mutation—are how we got here. But, for those who believe the Bible is life's literal blueprint, the evidence contradicts faith.

So they deny.

What happened in Dover is a tiny sliver, a broken shard of glass mirroring what plays out across the country. A war of fundamentalist Christian values versus secularism. A battle between evangelical fanaticism and tolerance.

And for those who must live in both worlds, we are caught in between.

As a reporter, I'm not supposed to care, not like this. I'm told I'm supposed to be able to set aside my feelings when I write stories.

But I am weary of hiding these feelings. I am weary of being told that I must treat everything as equal—evidence and faith, fact and fiction. I am weary of pretending this journey has led me nowhere, of the idea that I am merely a sponge that soaks up information and wrings it out again, leaving me dry and unchanged. I am weary of being judged, and accepting this judgment, because I'm supposed to believe it's given out of love and God's mercy.

My father owns a small storefront radio station twenty miles north of Dover that is dedicated to Christian fundamentalist programming. Each day, with unabashed earnestness, local evangelists deliver messages of Satan's lure, the evils of homosexuality, and the importance of converting the Jews.

Not too long ago, I walked into the radio station and listened to the voice of a man on air selling prayer closets for the impending Rapture. I stared at my father sitting behind his desk. Prayer closets? For the Rapture? Even this doesn't make him blink.

I'm not sure if the closets offer assurance that buyers will be taken up before the days of tribulation or if they merely offer protection and salvation after the Rapture takes place. But this much I know: There should be no need for prayer closets in a sane world.

I don't live in such a world. I look at my father and wonder how many other Americans are like him. Why are we so divided?

In Dover, those on the side of the truth weren't the ones marching under a banner of biblical fundamentalism and traditional values. "You can't lie for Jesus," I remind my father. No, the ones on the side of truth were the eleven parents who stood up to their local school board and said teaching their children about religion was their right, and not the job of the educational system.

But my father has closed his eyes to such a worldview. Rather, he wraps himself in his religion, retreating into a cocoon of denial. To him, the only thing that matters is whether I believe, whether I am saved.

So, once again, we play a game that we've been playing for ten years. A game that began when, in a fit of despair one night, overcome by failure and poverty and loneliness, my father dropped to his knees and begged for redemption.

"Are you a Christian?" he asks. And because I know the depth of his fears, I try to reassure him. But in the past year, I have changed. I can no longer deliver my carefully rehearsed lines with the same light touch.

"Yes," I try to say, "I'm a Christian." But this time, my tongue stumbles on the words.

And he knows. I'm the one lying now.

Three days earlier, I stood on the steps of Harrisburg's federal courthouse at the end of the trial of *Kitzmiller et al. v. Dover Area*

School District, trying to make sense of this swirl of emotions in my head. From a perch above the chaos, I watched the world clamor for a press conference. I wished my father had been there with me, so he could have witnessed what I saw. Maybe then he could understand.

Out the courthouse's back door, Dover board members slipped away, out of sight of the cameras and away from demanding questions. But on the courthouse's front steps, television crews from Germany and Japan and Italy pressed forward to listen to the parents and their lawyers.

The plaintiffs' lead attorney, Eric Rothschild, stood at the center. Only five feet five inches tall, Rothschild was lost amid the microphones. Unable to get to the center of the crowd, I climbed a wall off to the side and balanced on its ledge. Just below me, at my feet, a little girl with floppy brown curls struggled to climb up on the wall. Rothschild's ten-year-old daughter, Allison, wanted to see her father, but the crowd wasn't interested in little girls. She had been shoved to the back, just as I had been.

I reached down, grabbed Allison's hand, pulled her up in front of me. Stretching up on her tiptoes, she glanced, confused, back and forth between her mother below and her father in the crowd. We were both overwhelmed.

The federal courthouse is a white granite structure with wide-spaced steps leading up to the front doors. Everything was laid out like a stage. To my right, mostly hidden from view, the attorneys were pressed back against the courthouse, wide-eyed, dazed, and a little scared by the crush of attention. Scientists, forgotten by the press for the moment, stood on the steps in front of me, at center stage. Giddy with adrenaline, too little sleep, and far too much caffeine, they were playing with a panda puppet, a glib inside reference to the writings of Harvard evolutionary biologist Stephen Jay Gould. To my left, Steve Stough, one of the parents who had challenged the school board, watched. His head tilted back and his arms folded across his chest, Stough was beaming. I scribbled in my notebook, "Something beautiful played out here."

Later that day, I climbed into my car thinking about the news story I would write, wondering how I would do justice to what I had witnessed. But as I pulled out of the parking lot, the tears began. I tried to wipe them away with the back of my hand, but they kept coming. By the time I eased my car onto the highway crossing the Susquehanna River, I was sobbing.

I thought about calling my father. I'd fought with him almost every day of the trial. I'd wanted him to condemn, as a Christian, what seemed obvious to me to be deception. But he refused. I'd grow angry and hang up on him. The next day, I'd pick up the phone and try again. How do I explain to my father why this was so moving? How do I tell him we shouldn't be afraid of this? How can I describe what I witnessed?

I wanted him to know the parents' stories: Cyndi Sneath, who testified that she might not have a fancy education, but her eight-year-old son, Griffin, dreams of being an astronaut; of Bryan and Christy Rehm, who teach Bible school and sing in their church choir, but who were called atheists by their neighbors; and of Fred Callahan, a gentle, reserved man dismissed as intolerant. "What am I supposed to tolerate?" he asked. "The small encroachment of my First Amendment rights? Well, I'm not going to."

I wanted my father to understand Steve Harvey, one of the plaintiffs' attorneys and a dutiful Catholic who says we can only try to believe in God. On the morning of that last day of trial, he nervously paced around the block, smoking cigarettes and praying "Our Fathers."

Surely if my father were here, I thought, I could convince him. But not wanting to risk a fight, I didn't reach for the phone.

I thought there would be plenty of time to make my father understand.

Now, sitting in the Chinese restaurant, my father watching me from across the table, I realize that he never will.

My grandmother used to say to me, "Your problem, Lauri, is you're *schusslich*," using an old Pennsylvania Dutch word meaning scatterbrained. Now, more than ever, my head is bombarded as I try to make sense of everything that happened in the courtroom.

Because I can never remember, I dig into my food before my father can stop me. "Let us pray," he says. I put down my chopsticks and bow my head. We murmur grace over limp stir-fried green beans and lo mein smothered in duck sauce. I consider confessing that I am not a believer, but the waiter, once again topping off our water glasses, interrupts our conversation. We sit quietly. I keep my head down to avoid my father's frightened eyes, to avoid seeing how much he wants to save me from hell. But he leans forward across the table, catching my downward stare. He asks, "Are you searching for something?"

I guess I am, just not in the way he hopes. I shrug. Searching for a distraction, I open my fortune cookie. It says, "You have much skill in expressing yourself to be effective."

2

Neighbor Against Neighbor

In God have I put my trust; I will not be afraid what man can do unto me.

—*Psalm 56:11*

It's so familiar. Has anything changed in eighty years since the Scopes Monkey Trial? Or is what took place in Dover merely the latest incarnation of a battle waged by Christian fundamentalists since William Jennings Bryan prosecuted a young football coach for teaching evolution?

During the trial, when the out-of-town journalists ran out of scientists and lawyers and parents and pastors, they turned to the local reporters and asked, "Why Dover?"

I looked at them and struggled for answers. I usually said something about changing landscapes and suburbanization and newcomers moving into the area. I have never been satisfied with my response. This is because, as I struggled to come up with tidy conclusions, I realized the easy answers just aren't there. In Dover, at least, the pieces don't neatly fit together. "Darwinism"-spouting teachers were preachers' kids; the "atheist" plaintiffs taught Sunday school; the "activist" judge was a Bush-appointed Republican; and the journalists labeled "liars" were willing to go to jail for the truth. These people, along with school board members, administrators, pastors, lawyers, and scientists, uniquely contributed to what played out here.

Maybe, I've thought, it's the dirt. Dover sits at the edge of the Conewago Hills in Pennsylvania Dutch country. Part of York County, Dover is about twenty miles north of the Mason-Dixon Line, and about twenty miles south of the state capital of Harrisburg. Much of the area remains hidden far back from the main roads. Dover borough, the center of the Dover Area School District, has less than two thousand residents. But the district, which extends into the countryside, has a population of about twenty-four thousand. About one thousand students attend the high school.

A belt of red sandstone cuts through the district's hills, formed two hundred million years ago by grains of crushed quartz that have been washed downstream from once towering mountains. Poor German and English immigrants, unable to afford the more fertile limestone soil to the south, settled here. They pulled iron-rich red stone from heavy clay soil and used it to build houses and churches and schools. Like the soil, life was hard in this farming community.

In one family cemetery plot, under gravestones cut of this same sandstone, a sixteen-year-old mother lies next to her infant. The mother died in 1847, on the day her daughter was born. The baby joined her mother three months later.

Perhaps the years spent trying to build a life from the hard clay soil toughened these people and made them stubborn. Perhaps, in their isolation, they had evolved into a group of people who distrusted outsiders and resisted change.

But even as I talked to the media about Dover's history, I knew there was more to the story.

Some argue that what happened in Dover can only really be understood in the context of 9/11. Small events that occurred in the years following the terrorist attacks hardly seemed significant when considered individually. It's only when those events are strung together that a pattern emerges.

For the terrorist attacks didn't divide us. Not really. It was what came after that changed us. Briefly, for a few weeks, we had been drawn together as a nation united in grief. But what was seeded in 2001 was tended by men hungry for war. They told us that terrorists hate our freedoms. They warned us that you were either for us or against us. They exploited our fear and fueled our distrust of strangers. The world has changed, they said. We must be vigilant against unseen threats. In small towns such as Dover, people paid heed. They watched warily as new residents moved into subdivisions and strip malls sprouted where once there had been cornfields and cow pastures. They wondered where these outsiders were coming from.

Pastors who had once lectured on personal morality began preaching about the culture battles, about the war on religion. Tolerance became a sin, an abandonment of traditional values. Dover's students began to align themselves in terms of their faith—true believers and nonbelievers. They formed cliques based on what churches they attended. At my father's radio station, those witnessing for the Lord spoke of "taking back this nation as a Christian nation."

In the summer of 2002, Larry Reeser, a janitor and the district's head of building and maintenance, invited members of Dover's board of directors to visit their high school. Alan Bonsell, a newly elected member of the school board, came along on the tour.

During his election race, Bonsell campaigned on a platform of frugal spending and taxpayer reform. At the time, a controversial plan to renovate the high school angered many taxpayers. In the weeks leading up to his 2001 election, Bonsell spoke publicly of his commitment to education and public service. He outlined ideas for reining in spending on a project he and others dubbed the Taj Mahal.

But only weeks after taking his oath of office, he revealed another agenda. At a welcome meeting, administrators and members of the school board took turns addressing their ideas for the new year. One board member introduced plans for full-day kindergarten and block scheduling. Another discussed implementing a more consistent discipline policy and perhaps investing in a drug-sniffing dog. Bonsell spoke of creationism and school prayer.

A fundamentalist Christian, Bonsell believes that God shaped man from dust and breathed life into his lungs. In his mid-forties, Bonsell has a goatee and wide-spaced, feline blue eyes. With his sandy red hair, he looks a little bit like a lion. His wife, Brenda, tells him that he looks like Chuck Norris.

Only a few months before the school tour, Brenda completed treatment for breast cancer. Bonsell watched helplessly as the woman he considers his best friend suffered through a mastectomy and chemotherapy. It was the worst experience of his life, and only his faith sustained him. At night, Bonsell often stands at his windows, gazing at the stars, marveling at the intervening hand of God. "If you can't see that," he believes, "You're just not thinking critically."

On the tour, Reeser, the janitor nearing retirement, wanted school board members to see what children in Dover were being exposed to in science class.

Alone in the school that summer day, their footsteps carrying down the long hallway, Reeser led Bonsell, along with fellow board members Noel Wenrich and Jeff Brown, to the science wing. There, at the back of classroom No. 217, Reeser pointed to a painting balanced on the lip of the chalkboard.

For his senior graduation project, seventeen-year-old Zach

Strausbaugh painted a 4-by-16-foot mural of the Descent of Man and donated it to his favorite teacher. An easygoing kid, Strausbaugh wasn't particularly interested in science and he wasn't the best student, but he enjoyed painting. For months, he stayed after school, working alone on the project. The scene depicted an evolving line of our ape-like ancestors running across a savannah. It never occurred to him that there might be anything controversial about his work. After he graduated, Strausbaugh took a job at a graphic arts company. He pretty much forgot about the painting.

But Reeser couldn't forget. Each time he passed by the mural, he grew angrier, unable to keep himself from staring at the first ape's dangling genitalia.

"You can see the guy's *schwantz* hanging out," Reeser complained, using a Pennsylvania Dutch word for penis.

Board members looked at the painting and agreed that ape penises had no business in science class. But something else bothered Bonsell. A car radiator repairman with a business degree from nearby York College, Bonsell looked at the painting and snorted, disgusted that children were learning things in science class that contradicted the Bible, including the idea that humans evolved from apes. He grew up near Dover, the son of a moderately prosperous businessman. Bonsell owned his own shop and several apartment buildings. He sent his children to Dover schools. The family was well known in the community. Bonsell didn't like the changes that were overtaking his town. Children were becoming disrespectful, he believed. They wore baggy clothes with their underwear sticking out of their jeans. Bonsell interpreted what was happening as a decline of Christian values. He blamed it on God being taken out of the classroom.

At the time board members were eyeing the ape's *schwantz*, amazing strides were being made in decoding man's DNA. Scientists were rapidly completing the Human Genome Project, an intricate genetic road map of our ancestry. In addition to the scientific advances, that summer the Bush Administration pushed its campaign for an Iraq invasion. Many fundamentalists, in support, spoke reverently of the approaching Armageddon. "It's end times," my father told me.

Days before teachers returned from their summer break, Reeser carried the mural into the high school's parking lot. He set the student artwork on fire, watching the flames turn it to ashes.

After the 9/11 terrorist attacks, many Americans searched for proof that they had control over their existence, that the events weren't the result of random chaos. Many turned to Christ. About six months before Reeser set the mural on fire, in the beginning of 2002, Jane Cleaver, a seventy-four-year-old woman of Pennsylvania Dutch heritage, submitted a petition to Dover's school board.

"Public school prayer was taken away by one person in 1963," the petition read. "We the undersigned believe together we can put it back. On September 11, 2001, a horrible tragedy occurred at the New York [*sic*] Trade Center. Papers came home from our schools stating one of the ways we could help our children is to pray with them. If the school can condone prayer for a tragedy of such magnitude, couldn't it also condone prayer for an individual? We are petitioning the Dover Area School Board to allow prayer be put back into our Dover schools."

Fifteen hundred people signed their names to the petition, signatures gathered at churches throughout the district. Some, outsiders perhaps, might be tempted to write off the petition as representing the insular views of an isolated and rural population. But Cleaver's petition was similar to a proposed constitutional amendment sponsored by York County's Congressman Todd

Platts that would have legalized school prayer for the duration of the war on terror.[1] The amendment never made it to law. In Dover, the board appeased Cleaver by instituting a moment of silence in the school day, following the Pledge of Allegiance.

A year later, in January 2003, two board members quit amid an acrimonious fight over the high school renovation project. Bonsell called Cleaver and convinced her to join the board. He had known her since he was a boy. He used to buy candy at the 5-and-10 store she owned on Dover's Main Street. Even though Cleaver quit school in the eighth grade, Bonsell said she would be a good addition, touting her business success. The board also appointed Bill Buckingham, a fellow Christian fundamentalist and outspoken retired police officer and prison guard. Buckingham, in his late fifties, had been unable to work since suffering a back injury while breaking up a prison fight some twenty years earlier. To combat the chronic back pain he experienced from the injury, Buckingham had developed a then-secret addiction to the pain-killer OxyContin. But he bore his faith openly. On the lapel of his sportsjacket, he wore a pin in the shape of the Christian cross bearing an American flag. At the time, Buckingham was caring for his eighty-year-old father, who was dying of lung cancer. Three months after his appointment to the board, Buckingham and his wife, Charlotte, sat together as his father gurgled and gagged until, finally, he stopped fighting and took his last breath.

"I just felt so stinking helpless," Buckingham told me later of those hours next to his father's bed. "Here was my dad suffering and I couldn't do anything. I don't believe in euthanasia, but if he would have said, 'Shoot me,' God help me, I would have done it. We do that much for a damn dog. Why not a human being?"

Seeking reassurance, Buckingham asked doctors if his father had suffered in his final moments. But doctors couldn't give Buckingham what he needed. They could only say they didn't really know.

Buckingham admits this changed him. A year later, in March 2004, he checked himself into a rehabilitation treatment center for his OxyContin addiction.

Dover sits apart from York County's political machine. On election nights, the Democrats gather in the county seat of York at Sam & Tony's, a small storefront Italian restaurant, while the Republicans convene at the considerably more posh Yorktowne Hotel. But in the days before 2004, Dover candidates and their supporters usually waited out the results in their homes. Often, they just went to bed and would find out who won in the morning.

Still, most Dover school board members took their jobs seriously. Meetings were held twice a month at North Salem Elementary School in a brightly lit cafeteria painted with murals of dancing vegetables and cartons of milk. At long tables, board members debated the minutiae of educational matters with rigid adherence to parliamentary procedure. Often the debates became nasty and personal. Occasionally, a board member proposed adopting a policy that would promote Christianity, but fellow members always drew the line. Before he stepped down in 1999 to become a township supervisor, Alan Bonsell's father, Donald, had pushed unsuccessfully to have a Bible displayed prominently at all board meetings as a symbol for Christian guidance.

Still, despite their differences, board members, for the most part, were able to work together. They frequently shifted alliances based on their commitment to an issue, rather than their politics. When board member Casey Brown's husband, Jeff, replaced Donald Bonsell on the board, some assumed the couple would present a united front. In his first vote, Jeff Brown opposed his wife's meeting-schedule motion.

Following the 2001 election, the board tilted sharply right. Then, after Buckingham was appointed, what had been a series of isolated expressions of faith evolved into a closed-door campaign to restore God to the classroom.

Privately, Bonsell and Buckingham spoke of plans to require creationism to be taught alongside evolution. They complained to the school district's superintendent, Richard Nilsen, about the teaching of "monkey to man." They used taxpayer dollars to send Mike Baksa, the assistant superintendent, to a Christian college–sponsored conference on teaching creationism.

In closed-door planning meetings, Bonsell told administrators and board members he wanted the teaching of evolution to be balanced "50–50" with the teaching of creationism. He sat in Superintendent Nilsen's office and discussed his views about American history. He talked about his belief that America had been founded as a Christian nation and that nothing in the First Amendment precludes schools from teaching about God. Buckingham gave Nilsen a list of complaints he had about the ninth-grade biology textbook, including the fact that it contained a picture of Charles Darwin.

The science teachers whispered about the rumors they'd begun to hear that board members planned to target their biology curriculum. The teachers also knew, just as their colleagues across the country knew, that evolutionary theory had become an increasingly touchy subject because it contradicted the fundamentalist Christian worldview. Across the country, right-wing fundamentalist leaders rallied their constituency, emboldened by Bush's support of "faith-based" agendas.

Two of Dover's biology teachers, Jen Miller and Rob Eshbach, were children of pastors. They would never intentionally teach students to question their faith. But Miller and Eshbach, both dedicated professionals, knew evolutionary theory wasn't just some hunch. It was the foundation of modern biology. They knew there is more evidence supporting evolution than virtually any other scientific theory. While scientists may debate details of how the mechanism of evolution takes place, there is no legitimate scientific challenge to the theory.

Still, teachers were careful when dealing with students who'd been raised on the Bible and had been taught that acceptance of evolution shatters faith. When students challenged Eshbach in class, he invited them to come back after school. Then, in a quiet classroom, he told them how he is able to reconcile his knowledge of science with his belief in God. He was careful not to proselytize. Rather, he listened to their questions and answered them the best he could.

In his soft, measured cadence, Eshbach shared lessons learned from his father, a Lutheran pastor. He told them that he had been taught that Genesis was never meant to be a litmus test for faith. Rather, he said, he believed it was a story passed down from generation to generation, a beautiful human interpretation of our creation.

As a farmer who breeds beef cattle, Eshbach explained to students that he deals with the principles of natural selection every day. His scientific background has shown him that the Earth couldn't have been created in six days. He explained that he is not against faith, that faith guides him daily. The students didn't always agree, but they usually left reassured that, if nothing else, Eshbach certainly wasn't trying to demean their religion.

In class, Miller and Eshbach kept the discussion focused on evolution. If students continued to challenge them, as they sometimes did, with demands that they present other theories, the teachers told them to talk to their parents and pastors. They avoided the topic of humans and common descent. They brushed over the fossil record. Instead, they spent five days out of the school year lecturing on the concept of how small, incremental changes over time led to life's diversity.

Miller illustrated those changes by teaching about Darwin's finches. Charles Darwin, on his famed Galapagos expedition, noticed that the beaks of bird finches on islands with drier climates were larger and better adapted to nuts that thrived in the harsher conditions. Darwin theorized that over time, isolated from the mainland population, those finches became a new species through the process of natural selection. But while students could grasp the concept, they often became overwhelmed at humanity's relative blip of existence on Earth's awesome geological timeline. Miller took students out of class and stretched cash-register tape down the hallway. At her instruction, students labeled the different eons and eras and provided examples of life from each period. Miller carefully presented the information in a way that students could see that the age of the Earth made evolution possible.

Still, just as teachers do in other small towns, Miller and Eshbach stepped lightly over scientific truths in deference to the times. American science teachers, fearing religious backlash, have become timid about teaching evolutionary theory to their students.[2]

Looking back, Eshbach now wonders whether such deference was wise. In trying to appease the concerns of the community's many conservative Christians, perhaps they made themselves vulnerable to manipulation.

But at the time, few grasped what was happening either in Dover or across the country.

The sign taped to the front of science teacher Bertha Spahr's desk reads, "I sit on my golden throne and spew forth silver words of knowledge and you will learn."

Thirty years have passed, but former students, now middle-aged men and women with lined faces and thinning hair, can still recite those words from memory. And Eshbach himself remembers sitting in her classroom when he was a student seventeen years earlier, eyeing the urn next to her desk with a sign that said: "Ashes of problem students."

Spahr's message has always been clear. In her class, she's the boss. Back when she still could, she addressed smartass remarks with occasional slaps to the back of students' heads. But even without corporal punishment, the tiny woman commanded respect. Eshbach became a science teacher in part because of the education he received in Spahr's classroom.

When Spahr was a girl in the 1950s pondering her future, her Sicilian father told her she would go to college. She could major in medicine or science, he said. She chose science. When she started at Dover, she was one of only two female chemistry teachers in York County. The other was a nun at the local Catholic school.

Today, Spahr is the head of the district's science department and still teaches chemistry. She watches out for the teachers under her supervision with a protective, maternal spirit and they, in turn, are fiercely protective of her.

In the fall of 2002, Spahr stepped back into class to discover an empty space at the chalkboard where Zach Strausbaugh's mural used to be. She barged into the administration office, seeking an explanation. She was told to mind her own business.

Soon after, Bonsell met with Baksa, the assistant superintendent, to talk about creationist claims against evolution. Bonsell wanted biology teachers to teach those claims, even though the scientific community gives no credence to them. He argued there were huge gaps in the fossil record. He talked about the Piltdown Man, a 1912 discovery in a British quarry that some speculated at the time could be man's "missing link." Creationists frequently point to the fact that the Piltdown Man was later determined to be a fraud, as an example that the evidence for man's evolutionary history is a hoax. But scientists point out that one false claim doesn't discount the rest of the fossil evidence, which, despite Bonsell's misguided belief, is extensive.

Baksa, caught in the middle, visited the science teachers' classes over lunch. He related Bonsell's concerns. He told them about Bonsell's plan that creationism should be taught alongside evolution. Bryan Rehm, a physics teacher, laughed at Baksa before realizing the man wasn't joking. Teachers began asking questions about what they were hearing. In a memo, Dover's principal, Trudy Peterman, asked about the creationist conversations and challenged the administration. Nilsen, the superintendent, dismissed the woman, saying she had a habit of exaggerating, and later he gave her a bad performance review.

The teachers grew increasingly alarmed. Rehm, no longer amused, sensed where things were going. Though board members hadn't targeted his physics curriculum, Rehm saw the gathering storm as an attack on academic freedom. He often went home at the end of the day and ranted to his wife, Christy, an English teacher in a neighboring district. At first, Christy was unconcerned. The Rehms often talk shop, holding long discussions about education and policy. When Bryan got frustrated, he frequently launched into sarcastic rapid-fire tirades. But as the months passed, Christy began to hear bitterness creep into her husband's rants.

Bonsell, meanwhile, grew tired of sending administrators to meet with teachers and met with them himself. During one of the meetings, Jen Miller sat across from Bonsell and nervously assured him that the chapter she taught on evolution only covered "change over time." She told him that they didn't teach about origins of life, but rather origins of species.

Bonsell told the teachers that his daughter would be taking biology that year and he didn't want her learning about human evolution. He told them that he was concerned that teachers could be accused of lying to students if they taught them something that contradicted their faith.

The teachers understood Bonsell's message. Teaching evolution could be dangerous. Fearing retribution, Miller stopped using the timeline in the hallway and began teaching solely from the textbook.

While board members only spoke privately of their desire to inject creationism into science class, occasionally they hinted at their religious motives in public. In the fall of 2003, as the U.S. Supreme Court was about to review the constitutionality of the phrase "under God" in the Pledge of Allegiance, the newly appointed Buckingham urged the board to adopt a resolution in support of the two words.

Buckingham's behavior that night foreshadowed what would take place half a year later. He argued that this country was founded on Christianity. People of other faiths were free to come to this country and worship any way they liked, he said, but if they begin to infringe on the country's "Christian values," they should go back to where they came from.

Over the next few months, Buckingham, as head of the district curriculum committee, and Bonsell, now president of the school board, turned their attention to the purchase of a new biology book. Unhappy with any book that taught students about evolution, Buckingham gave Superintendent Nilsen two DVDs put out by the Discovery Institute, an organization that advocates for intelligent design. In the DVD *Icons of Evolution*, writer Jonathan Wells criticizes many aspects of evolutionary theory, including the idea that natural selection could be responsible for the change of one species into another over time. In *Unlocking the Mystery of Life*, creationist Dean Kenyon makes the case for intelligent design through a discussion of the complexity of DNA.

At the end of the 2003–2004 school year, as teachers prepared for summer vacation, Assistant Superintendent Baksa asked them to watch the movies in between packing up books and papers. Bryan Rehm watched a few minutes and was disgusted by how the documentaries misrepresented the scientific facts. He polished up his resume and began to look for a job outside Dover.

Looking back, Barrie Callahan says she can't believe how naïve she was that she didn't see it coming. Before she joined the school board, Callahan took it for granted that people accepted evolution. Then she spent ten years as a board member, listening to her colleagues rail about the demise of Christian values. She tries to sift through her memory, but the remarks about prayer and the Bible and creationism run together and she is unable to pick out specific conversations. But she hasn't forgotten their views.

"They're a mystery to me," she recalls. "I've never been around people like that."

Then, in June 2004, the behind-closed-doors discussions of creationism were finally aired at two public meetings that would become central to Dover's battle over intelligent design. It started at the June 7 meeting, when Callahan stood up and asked when the ninth-grade students were going to get new biology textbooks. For the past couple of years, there had been too few books to go around. Students were forced to share copies.

Callahan is a tiny, tanned woman with blond curls that frame her heart-shaped face. A mother of three, she's warm and energetic, passionate and giggly. Many school board members couldn't stand her, perhaps because of her willingness to express her views. One of her former colleagues described her as "bitchy." Her husband, Fred, a paper company executive, adores her.

Callahan asked the same question each month since she lost her reelection bid in 2002 over the school construction issue. She knew what was behind board members' reluctance to buy the science textbooks. Callahan also knew that her persistence, and their personal dislike of her, would eventually lead them to say publicly what they had been whispering privately.

Buckingham, as head of the curriculum committee, told Callahan that he refused to approve the purchase of the book because it was "laced with Darwinism."

Callahan threw up her hands and said what she already knew. "Great. So this is about evolution?"

Buckingham said he wanted a textbook that was balanced by the inclusion of creationism.

Those present that night remember hearing gasps of surprise from the public. Board member Jeff Brown looked out into the audience and saw two local newspaper reporters, Joe Maldonado of the *York Daily Record* and Heidi Bernhard-Bubb of the *York Dispatch*, scribbling furiously. Brown groaned to himself and envisioned the next day's headlines. Brown waited for Bonsell, as board president, to point out that teaching creationism is inappropriate in science class. But rather than contradict Buckingham's idea, Bonsell, along with another board member Noel Wenrich, spoke in favor of it. Bonsell argued it was possible to teach creationism without it being religion.

Max Pell, a Dover graduate and a Penn State freshman, sat in the audience that night. He hadn't come to speak but to see his girlfriend, who was a student representative and shared a seat at the table with board members. But Pell was shocked. He took his turn at the podium. Politely, he warned board members that teaching creationism in public school violated the First Amendment. Buckingham looked at the young man. "Have you ever heard of brainwashing?" Buckingham asked Pell. "If students are taught only evolution, it stops becoming theory and becomes fact."

A week later, at the June 14 meeting, the elementary school cafeteria was filled. People who had never attended a meeting before sat in the audience, concerned after reading newspaper accounts of the proposal to teach creationism.

Buckingham started the meeting with an apology. But rather than temper his previous remarks, he said he couldn't censor himself in the interest of being politically correct. "Nowhere in the Constitution does it call for a separation of church and state," he said.

He spoke of liberals in "black robes" taking away the rights of Christians. He challenged residents to "trace your roots to the monkey you came from."

Residents of the small town stepped to the podium. The line stretched to the back of the room, looping behind the folding metal chairs. Some spoke in support of teaching creationism. Some talked about putting God back in school. Buckingham's wife, Charlotte, read from the book of Genesis. She said people needed to become "born again." She asked, "How can we teach anything else?" as board members murmured "Amen." To a horrified Casey Brown, it felt like her fellow board members were hosting a tent revival.

But others urged the school board to think about what they were suggesting. Bertha Spahr, as head of the science department, told them that teachers tried to be sensitive to creationist views. They recommended purchasing the Prentice Hall–published textbook *Biology* because, Spahr said, it was "the least offensive book we could find."

Buckingham dismissed her concerns. "Two thousand years ago, someone died on the cross," he said. "Won't somebody stand up for him?"

Christy Rehm watched, aghast, from the back of the room, nine months pregnant and uncomfortable sitting on a metal chair. She had come at her husband's behest. She heard Buckingham tell Maldonado, "This country wasn't founded on Muslim beliefs or evolution. This country is founded on Christianity, and our students should be taught as such."

Christy's students come from different religious backgrounds. Though she's a Christian, she'd never forced her beliefs on them. Wouldn't it be awful, she thought, to teach students that only her brand of Christianity was right and everyone else was wrong?

The Reverend Warren Eshbach sat quietly listening to the back-and-forth arguments. Earlier that day, he had looked out his window and seen his youngest son, Rob, the soft-spoken teacher, stride up the sidewalk, and thought he had come for a visit or to catch him up on his grandchildren. But Rob Eshbach, fearing that board members planned to attack the science curriculum, had come to ask him to attend the meeting. He knew his father's strengths at conflict resolution. In Baltimore in the 1960s, he organized civil rights marches and worked to unite the community at a time when racism and riots were tearing it apart.

At the meeting, Pastor Eshbach stood up and addressed the board. He begged them not to do what he feared they were about to do. He warned them they would only divide the town. He warned them they would turn neighbor against neighbor.

3

Met on the Battlefield

That God intervened in the supernatural way to gather the animals into the ark and to keep them under control during the year of the flood is explicitly stated in the text of scripture. Furthermore, it is obvious that the opening of the windows of heaven in order to allow the waters which were above the firmament to fall upon the earth, and the breaking up of all the bounties of the great deep, were supernatural acts of God.
— John Whitcomb and Henry Morris, The Genesis Flood:
The Biblical Record and Its Scientific Implications

The Thomas More Law Center pledges to be the sword and shield for Christians. Named after the Catholic patron saint of lawyers, the firm is based in Ann Arbor, Michigan. Domino's Pizza millionaire Thomas Monaghan, a devout Catholic, and Richard Thompson, a former Oakland County, Michigan, prosecutor, founded the organization in 1999. Using the courts as its battlefield, the not-for-profit's goal is to lead a revolution against secular society.

Thompson is best known for his repeated attempts to convict assisted-suicide proponent Jack Kevorkian of murder. Finally voters, fed up with the expense of his quixotic mission, threw him out of office. (The prosecutor who took office after Thompson would charge Kevorkian with second-degree murder and successfully convict him.)

The Thomas More Law Center's mission statement says, "Our ministry was inspired by the recognition that the issues of the cultural war being waged across America, issues such as abortion, pornography, school prayer, and the removal of the Ten Commandments from municipal and school buildings, are not being decided by elected legislatures, but by the courts."

Thompson, a man of passionate views, often speaks of the "moral relativism" that he believes defines this nation's culture, a phenomenon he blames on Charles Darwin. "Darwinism," as he refers to evolutionary theory, removes the fear of divine retribution and allows us to live as "Godless atheists."

Because intelligent design invokes the supernatural, it fits well with an evangelical worldview. The concept is based on the idea that design in specific organisms can be detected. Intelligent design's proponents say they can't identify the designer, only that the organism was designed. But it's pretty clear that when people talk about a designer, they're talking about God.

Thompson was eager for an intelligent design battle his law firm could take to the U.S. Supreme Court. Robert Muise, an attorney with the law firm, had been assigned to find one. Whenever an evolution controversy erupted in a district somewhere in the country, he'd visit the school board and lobby its members to adopt intelligent design as part of their biology curriculums.

In May 2000, he visited Charleston, West Virginia. Karl Priest, a middle-school mathematics teacher, had been trying to get members of the Kanawha County school board to adopt *Of Pandas and People*, an intelligent design textbook, into their science curriculum.

Muise, an earnest and boyish-looking man in his late thirties, stood before the board at a public meeting and said that intelligent design wasn't a religious concept. He assured board members that it was based on sound empirical evidence.

Still, they would undoubtedly be sued, Muise told them. In exchange for their willingness to be foot soldiers in the culture wars, the Thomas More Law Center would defend them for free.

"We'll be your shield against such attacks," Muise told skeptical board members. The board members listened politely, but declined the offer.

In many ways, what happened in West Virginia paralleled Dover's introduction to intelligent design. The movement appeared to be led by a grassroots coalition. It was started by people who claimed that their sole interest was to improve science education. They said they merely wanted students to learn both sides of what they called the scientific controversy. At some point, outsiders came to town, offering assistance. However, one major difference existed between Dover's school board and Kanawha's. Those in West Virginia recognized that the designer was God and believed that religion had no place in science class. John Luoni, the former president of the Kanawha school board, followed Dover's battle in the newspapers. He was surprised when he learned that board members had accepted the law firm's offer.

As in Dover, Luoni said that residents of his school district are, by and large, churchgoers. He is a Methodist and attends service regularly. "We're certainly not anti-religious," he said in a soft West Virginia drawl. Some schools still hold Christmas pageants. Occasionally, he said, they probably even slip a few Christmas carols into the program.

But Luoni, who is an engineer, said, "We believe we needed to have the best scientific theories taught in science class."

At what point did outside interest groups first reach out to Dover? The question of timing is significant because it might reveal whether this was a national war playing out in a small town, or a small-town political battle that played out on the national stage.

Did Dover's school board members inadvertently step into a debate raging across the country, only to be exploited by activist attorneys more interested in promoting their agenda than in looking out for Dover's students and taxpayers? Or were Buckingham and Bonsell so convinced of their cleverness that they believed their actions would stand up to the scrutiny of a federal judge? Perhaps it was some combination of the two—a perfect storm of audacity.

The few individuals who know for sure won't say. The rest of us can only guess.

But this much is known: At some point that summer, Buckingham spoke with someone at the Thomas More Law Center.

Today, Buckingham says his memory has faded. When pressed to recall key details, he speaks of his painkiller addiction and the memory problem it caused. He cannot remember when he spoke with either organization, he says, or who picked up the phone and contacted whom first.

But Jeff and Casey Brown say that some contact was made in between the two June board meetings. In a closed-door executive session before the second public meeting, Buckingham said he talked to a Thomas More lawyer. Attorneys there had read about Dover's creationism debate and had offered assistance, just as they did with other school boards across the country. Buckingham described intelligent design as a scientific version of creationism. He said the textbook *Of Pandas and People* could be used in place of *Biology.*

At the time, Jeff Brown knew almost nothing about intelligent design, but he thought it sounded like a cool concept. "I didn't understand what it was," he explained later.

At the end of June, Barrie Callahan, who brought out school board members' ire, ran into Baksa, the assistant superintendent, at the high school.

"They said creationism," she gushed, excited that board members had finally, publicly, on the record, revealed their religious motivations. They talked of getting creationism into science class in a room filled with close to one hundred people. They said it in front of two newspaper reporters. Their words had been tape-recorded. Callahan was elated, but Baksa warned her that the fight might not be over.

At the July school board meeting, Bonsell and Buckingham stopped talking about creationism. Instead, they started talking about intelligent design.

Joe Maldonado, a stringer for the *Daily Record*, where I also worked, noticed an abrupt shift in tone. Somewhere between June and July, board members' demeanor changed. It became, Maldonado remembers, "a whole lot less Christian and a lot more scientific sounding. They were no longer talking about taking a stand for Jesus. It was about taking a stand for our children's education."

After the meeting, Maldonado approached Bonsell. The two men spoke casually. Maldonado asked Bonsell to explain intelligent design.

Bonsell said it was a scientific theory, an alternative to Darwinism. It was the idea, he said, of "something designed intelligently."

Maldonado visited the *Daily Record*'s newsroom the following day. He paused at my desk and we chatted about the news. As at many newspapers, the reporters who cover small-town school board meetings are typically correspondents. Rather than receiving a weekly salary, they are independent contractors and are paid by the story. Often they have other jobs or are retirees or housewives seeking a little extra income. As a correspondent, Maldonado had been covering Dover for years. He lives in the district and knows the people well. As a boy growing up in York County, he was the child of a Puerto Rican mother and an absent Italian father. He is a devout Baptist and makes no attempt to hide his faith. He homeschools his teenage special-needs son and runs a sandwich stand at the farmers' market in York.

Maldonado also writes poetry. His poems reveal sentiments of spirituality and love and fear and sex so unguarded that at his book readings, it's sometimes hard to listen without looking down in shyness. He is the most innocently honest person I have ever met.

Buckingham knew of Maldonado's faith. Before he sought treatment for his OxyContin addiction, he called Maldonado and confided his demons. Buckingham told him he trusted him because he was a Christian. But Maldonado is also a journalist. To him, Christianity isn't some fraternity in which he grants preferential treatment to those in the club. "Just because I'm a Christian," he warned board members, "I'm not going to cut anybody any slack."

As the education reporter, I was watching Dover's battle closely. We chatted at my desk and I asked Maldonado if board members were still talking about creationism. He described their discussion about intelligent design. It intrigued me. In the concept, I thought I recognized the intervening hand of the divine.

Scientific proof of the existence of God? Is such a thing possible? If so, it could give me what I desperately crave. I cannot count the number of times I've sat on cold, hard folding chairs in Pentecostal church services, witnessing the faithless find redemption. I've sung His praises—Isn't he wonderful? Wonderful, isn't he?—to the rhythm of jangling tambourines and thumping electric bass.

I listened to the sobs of jubilation as my father, slain in the spirit, brought the burdened forward to the pulpit.

I watched uncomfortably as he delivered salvation to kneeling sinners, gently pressing his hand to earnest, upward-tilted faces, watching as they collapsed in euphoria and relief. I watched and pretended I needed no such salvation. I assured the church brethren that I already believed. I glared at them when they asked if I had been saved, daring them to challenge me, to judge me. I spoke the right words, but I knew my father would have loved nothing more than to confront me, to force me to come out as a lost soul seeking God's mercy. Fortunately, he never tried.

The truth is, despite my religious ambivalence, I envy people of faith. I picture their sleep so different from my own—secure, uninterrupted by fear and doubt, unspoiled by images of our mortality.

How many hours have I spent awake in my own bed, my slumbering husband next to me, watching the sky turn from black to dawn? When my sons were young, and I would awake at night, I'd pad into their rooms and throw extra blankets on them.

My sons are older now and in college. And now I lie in bed helpless, wondering, are they driving somewhere right now? Are they wearing their seatbelts? Are they safe? My father, after he became saved, spoke often of the need to cover his children with blankets, of wrapping us in salvation.

Proof of the existence of God? How wonderful! With Maldonado still standing at my desk, I did the same thing many in Dover were doing. I turned to my computer's search engine, and typed in the words "intelligent design."

By the time August arrived at North Salem Elementary, the floors were polished free of scuff marks, windows wiped clean of smeared nose prints. At the school board meeting that month,

Buckingham argued in favor of adopting *Pandas* as a supplemental textbook to the Prentice Hall textbook *Biology*. Written by creationists Percival Davis and Dean H. Kenyon, the book's full title is *Of Pandas and People: The Central Question of Biological Origins.* Published by the Texas-based Foundation for Thought and Ethics, an organization whose stated purpose is to make "known the Christian gospel and understanding of the Bible and the light it sheds on the academic and social issues of our day," it's touted as the first pro–intelligent design textbook. It was released in 1989, two years after the Supreme Court's blow to creation science in *Edwards v. Aguillard,* when it ruled that the concept was religion and could not be taught in public school science classes.

Buckingham had lined up enough votes, and he threatened to block the purchase of *Biology* if the other board members didn't agree to buy *Pandas.* Barely a month earlier, board members eyed spending cuts and slashed the library budget in half. Now, they were debating whether to spend extra money for a nonrequired textbook. At first, the board split 4–4 in favor of buying the Prentice Hall book; Bonsell did not take Buckingham's side. A nasty argument ensued, and the tie was broken only after board member Angie Yingling changed her vote, swayed by the argument that students should have their copies of *Biology* in time for the new school year. A furious Buckingham vowed that the fight wasn't over.

Publicly the pro–intelligent design board members now spoke only of their commitment to improving education and challenging children to think critically by presenting alternative views. But Jeff and Casey Brown remembered them speaking in executive sessions of leading a Christian revolution.

In curriculum committee meetings, Buckingham led his group in discussions of ways to sneak Christ's teachings into school. He assigned Baksa, the assistant superintendent, to research the teaching of evolution at private Christian schools. Baksa, once his report was completed, handed board members a list of creationist textbooks and an outline of Christian alternatives to evolutionary theory, including young earth creationism, old earth creationism, and intelligent design.

Steve Russell, the district's regular attorney, warned Dover officials against embarking on their religious pursuit. Russell knew these people well and understood what they were considering. His wife, dying of cancer, was the board secretary and had been seated next to them at public meetings twice a month for more than a decade. Russell knew their Christian beliefs. And he knew what they really meant when they talked about improving education by presenting alternative theories to evolution.

He sent them an e-mail warning them it would be a mistake. He reminded them that they had already revealed their intentions to get God in science class. He told them that if they insisted on pursuing their intelligent design policy, they would undoubtedly be sued. And, he warned, they would lose.

The Dover school board members were unimpressed. They told Russell not to bother coming to meetings anymore. They had a plan.

As board members quietly plotted, 2,700 miles away, a group of about twenty-five scientists and lawyers gathered at a hotel conference center in San Francisco.

Just as Thomas More Law Center searched for a school district to embrace intelligent design, the scientists and lawyers who were gathered on the West Coast were also looking for a possible test case. Americans United for Separation of Church and State attended the meeting, along with Ohio's American Civil Liberties Union (ACLU), which had been busy that year fending off creationist attempts to get intelligent design into state education standards. The event was hosted by the National Center for Science Education (NCSE), an organization created in 1983 to defend the teaching of evolution from religious attacks. Among those there were NCSE's executive director Eugenie Scott, along with newly hired public information officer Nick Matzke.

Raised a Lutheran, Matzke has undergraduate degrees in chemistry and biology and a master's degree in geography. He wears wire-rimmed glasses and has a moon face. He hunts elk each year with his family in Oregon and dresses like an outdoorsman. When forced to dress up, he typically wears a prep-school uniform of khaki pants and Navy sports jackets. His interest in the battle against evolution was piqued as a child reading the creationist tracts sent to him by his fundamentalist grandmother, a woman he adored.

Eugenie Scott is a willowy fifty-eight-year-old anthropologist with oversized eyeglasses, a pale complexion, and a wicked sense of humor. She became the NCSE's director the same year as the *Aguillard* decision, trading in her science career to defend the teaching of evolution.

More than almost anyone, Scott understands how creationists were redefining themselves. Following each defeat, she watched as they distanced themselves from their biblical literalism and adopted more sophisticated guises to step around constitutional church-and-state barriers. Scott was on the front lines when creationism morphed into creation science. And she was watching as creation science shape-shifted into intelligent design.

Those at the meeting noted the increasing grassroots popularity of intelligent design, a concept that, along with *Pandas*, emerged in the wake of *Edwards v. Aguillard*.

Sitting in the hotel conference room, Scott, Matzke, and others ran down the list of creationist flare-ups across the country. In 1999, the Kansas State Board of Education drew national attention when its members deleted evolution from the state's science stan-dards. The state's citizens disagreed with the board's actions. In the next election, board members who had voted for the change were defeated, and evolution was restored.

But rather than go away, the issue reemerged in Kansas and appeared in other states. In the previous few years, attacks on evolution had increased significantly.[1] At the time that Dover was revising its biology curriculum, similar challenges were taking place in twelve other states.[2]

Fundamentalist fervor fanned across the country the summer of 2004. With the presidential election only months away, Christian right leaders mobilized their base. On Sunday mornings, preach-ers such as Jerry Falwell gave barely disguised political speeches, cloaking them in sermons. They touted President Bush's cam-paign of "family values." Evangelicals believed that classroom attacks on evolution might be ready to pass constitutional muster.

Those gathered in San Francisco wanted an intelligent design test case, just as the Thomas More Law Center did. But the case they envisioned would strike a devastating blow, exposing intelli-gent design as the latest incarnation of creation science. Someone in the room asked about what had been brewing in Dover.

In late August, Dover was only a tiny blip on their radar, over-shadowed by bigger stories in Kansas and Ohio. But what was playing out there intrigued those in the room. They discussed the possibilities and agreed that Dover had just about everything. There was little ambiguity. Board members had clearly broadcast their religious motivations with public discussions of creationism at the June meetings. They had already talked about adopting *Pandas*, a textbook with a creationist history. A court challenge would take place in Pennsylvania, where courts might be less hos-tile to science than in the more conservative South.

Founded by Quakers, Pennsylvania was built on the concept

of religious tolerance. With the exception of Rhode Island, its Constitution possesses a religious freedom provision far more liberal than those of the other thirteen original colonies. Section 4 states,

> All men have a natural and indefeasible right to worship Almighty God according to the dictates of their own consciences; no man can of right be compelled to attend, erect or support any place of worship, or to maintain any ministry against his consent; no human authority can, in any case whatever, control or interfere with the rights of conscience, and no preference shall ever be given by law to any religious establishments or modes of worship.

If Dover's school board were to continue its push to force intelligent design into the curriculum, those in San Francisco concluded, it could be a dream come true—the perfect test case.

Another national organization, this one based in Seattle, was also watching developments in Dover. At first, members of the Discovery Institute's Center for Science and Culture supported Dover's criticism of evolution. At least that's how Buckingham remembers it.

Members of the pro–intelligent design organization sent videos to the school district and encouraged board members, Buckingham says. But amid fears of a lawsuit, they backed off from pushing for teaching intelligent design and suggested instead a watereddown approach of "teach-the-controversy" of evolution.

While the Discovery Institute touts itself as being at the forefront of what it calls a debate over "neo-Darwinism," the organization is actually part of creationists' long-evolving struggle dating back eighty years. In 1925, America was embroiled in a culture war. Prohibition had been passed six years earlier at the behest of religious conservatives. Darwin's theories, despite initial resistance, had gained general public acceptance. But in the 1920s, a fundamentalist movement began to flourish, mostly in the poor and rural South. The Scopes Monkey Trial emerged from this zeitgeist, catching the attention of the nation.

John Scopes stood accused of violating the Butler Act, a Tennessee law stating that no teacher in a publicly funded school may "teach any theory that denies the story of the Divine Creation of man as taught in the Bible, and to teach instead that man has descended from a lower order of animals."

Following the passage of the Butler law, the newly formed American Civil Liberties Union searched for a case to challenge it. The ACLU ran advertisements in Tennessee newspapers, offering to represent anyone accused of teaching evolution. A Dayton businessman saw the ads and convinced community leaders that a court case would be great publicity for the town. Scopes, a football coach and substitute teacher, was enlisted to help, even though he couldn't actually remember teaching evolution to students.

It was the first time the teaching of evolution had been challenged in the courts. But because Judge John T. Raulston would not permit scientific testimony during the trial, he hampered the defense from making a case that creationism was not legitimate science. The ACLU-backed Clarence Darrow initially pursued the case as a violation of First Amendment church-and-state protections. But as the case progressed, he switched strategies and argued that there was no conflict between the Bible and evolutionary theory. The trial is remembered for the great intellectual showdown between Darrow and William Jennings Bryan, an ardent populist who defended Tennessee's anti-evolution statute based on his belief that "social Darwinism" had been used to exploit the poor and working classes in the post–World War I turmoil.[3]

Though he was the lead prosecutor, Bryan took the stand to defend a literal interpretation of the Bible. During his testimony, he accused Darrow of trying "to cast ridicule on everybody who believes in the Bible." Darrow responded, "We have the purpose of preventing bigots and ignoramuses from controlling the education of the United States."

Columnist H. L. Mencken covered the trial, filing caustic dispatches for the *Baltimore Evening Sun*, a newspaper fifty miles south of Dover. In his June 29 column, "Homo Neanderthalensis," Mencken wrote,

> Every step in human progress, from the first feeble stirrings in the abyss of time, has been opposed by the great majority of men. Every valuable thing that has been added to the store of man's possessions has been derided by them when it was new, and destroyed by them when they had the power. They have fought every new truth ever heard of, and they have killed every truth-seeker who got into their hands.

It was a fascinating case, but what is often forgotten in the story is that Scopes lost. Judge Raulston fined him one hundred dollars.

While his conviction was later overturned on a legal technicality—in Tennessee, the jury was supposed to set the amount of the fine, not the judge—the teaching of evolutionary theory languished in the decades following the trial. Those who opposed evolution didn't disappear for eight decades, only to reappear in Dover. Rather, many communities passed laws that prohibited the teaching of any science that contradicted the Bible.

In 1965, Susan Epperson, a twenty-four-year-old Little Rock biology teacher, sued the Arkansas public school system, challenging a state law that prohibited the teaching of evolution. Three years later, the U.S. Supreme Court sided with Epperson, determining that the sole reason for the anti-evolution law was that fundamentalist Christians believed the theory conflicted with Genesis.

To creationists today, Epperson is a pariah. At the Answers in Genesis Museum just outside of Cinncinnati, a place devoted to the idea that the Bible is the only true science textbook, a grafitti-covered "hall of shame" stands dedicated to the changes that have taken place since her victory. The trash-strewn hallway features exhibits about gay marriage and the Columbine massacre.

But Epperson's First Amendment challenge was not the only blow to the creationist movement. The Russians' 1957 launch of *Sputnik* into outer space had contributed to a change in the national mood. New anti-communist fears fueled a demand for better science education.

In response, creationists evolved. Led by Henry Morris, the founder of the Institute for Creation Research, they revamped their arguments in an attempt to disguise the fact that their beliefs were based on religion. The repackaged result was "creation science," which disputes the conventional geological timetable and claims that evidence shows that the earth is six thousand years old. It argues that the Genesis account of Noah's ark is supported by "flood geology," which claims that a global flood was caused by water emerging from fissures in the earth and a pink canopy of vapor in the atmosphere.

The courts didn't buy it. In decisions such as *McLean v. Arkansas* and *Edwards v. Aguillard*, they struck down the concept as merely a disingenuous attempt to attack evolution and force God into science class. In his sharply worded opinion in the 1982 *McLean* case, Judge William R. Overton set the legal parameters for science that would guide attorneys years later in a Harrisburg courtroom.

Overton defined the essential characteristics of science: "It must be guided by natural law; it has to be explanatory by reference to natural law; it is testable against the empirical world; its conclusions are tentative, that is, not necessarily the final word; it is falsifiable." The existence of God, for instance, is an unfalsifiable hypothesis. Overton concluded that because creationism failed to meet the criteria, it could not be taught in science classes as science.

Because the *McLean* decision was never appealed, it had no legal standing outside Arkansas. A few years later, creationists tried again. This time they passed a law in Louisiana called the Balanced Treatment for Creation-Science and Evolution-Science in Public School Instruction Act, which required equal time for both approaches.

This time the case, *Edwards v. Aguillard*, was appealed to the U.S. Supreme Court. After the 1987 *Aguillard* ruling against creation science, which ruled that Louisiana's balanced treatment act was unconstitutional, creationists' arguments evolved further. This time, they came up with intelligent design.

At its heart, intelligent design is simply a reworking of British philosopher William Paley's two-hundred-year-old "watchmaker" analogy. A person walking through a field stumbles upon a watch. It is carefully assembled and wouldn't function without all its parts working together. The person's inevitable conclusion? The watch must have a maker. Since living organisms are far more complex than a watch, Paley reasoned that if a watch had to be designed, certainly the far greater complexities of a living organism—a mouse, for instance—would have to have been designed.

"The marks of design are too strong to be got over," Paley wrote in his book *Natural Theology*. "Design must have had a designer. That designer must have been a person. That person is God."

★   ★   ★

In 1987, the same year of the *Aguillard* decision, University of California, Berkeley, law professor Phillip Johnson was on sabbatical in England. Each morning, he passed by a science bookstore on his walk to his University College office. Looking in the shop window, he noticed two books: Michael Denton's *Evolution: A Theory in Crisis*, and Richard Dawkins' *The Blind Watchmaker*. A born-again Christian, Johnson had been searching for a mission, a purpose for his life. After reading the books, he decided his mission would be to destroy the materialistic worldview of evolutionary theory.

He concluded that the decisions in *McLean* and *Aguillard*, both of which rejected the two-model approach of teaching creationism as an alternative to evolution, closed the door on God. In order to level the playing field, he realized, creationists needed to first destroy the principles of science, in order to make room for the supernatural in scientific study. (Because supernatural causes can never be disproved, scientific study limits observation and study solely to the natural world—a concept known as methodological naturalism.)

In his book *Darwin on Trial*, published in 1991 by the Christian-based InterVarsity Press, Johnson described his realization. "The academy does define science in such a way that advocates of supernatural creation may neither argue for their own position nor dispute the claims of the scientific establishment."

The process of science, he decided, needed to be changed to accommodate the supernatural. He proposed a "Big Tent" attack similar to Ronald Reagan's model for the Republican Party. In order to get God into science class, creationists needed to tone down their rhetoric. Rather than argue that the earth is six thousand years old and that the fossil record was created by the Great

Flood, intelligent design proponents should take no official position on those issues, Johnson argued, focusing instead on changing the very definition of science.

In 1993, Johnson invited future leaders of the intelligent design movement to a conference in the California beach town of Pajaro Dunes. Michael Behe, William Dembski, Jonathan Wells, Kurt Wise, and Paul Nelson joined him.[4] Nelson later wrote about Johnson's strategy, "The promise of the big tent of ID is to provide a setting where Christians and others may disagree amicably and fruitfully about how best to understand the natural world as scripture."

But Johnson also outlined a more ambitious plan, one he said is based on John 1:1. The New Testament verse guides fundamentalist Christian beliefs. Without a literal interpretation of the Old Testament, one cannot accept the truth of Christ: "In the beginning was the Word, and the Word was with God, and the Word was God."[5]

Johnson said he wanted to create a new world based on fundamentalist Christian beliefs. The first step would be to drive a wedge into society's "scientific materialism."[6]

Three years after the meeting in 1996, the Discovery Institute founded its Center for Renewal of Science and Culture, ostensibly to develop the concept of intelligent design. Many of the same people at the conference became fellows at the Seattle organization, including Johnson, Behe, and Dembski.

Discovery's initial letterhead, brochures, and website featured Michelangelo's painting in the Sistine Chapel depicting God touching Adam. A later banner still featured God but replaced Adam with a double helix of DNA. It changed its name from "Center for Renewal of Science and Culture" to simply the "Center for Science and Culture."

Its members vehemently deny the organization's creationist

links, but despite attempts to hide their true motivations, Discovery fellows have made repeated statements that reveal their intended purpose. As Dembski said in an interview in *Touchstone*, a Christian magazine, "Intelligent design is just the Logos theology of John's Gospel restated in the idiom of information theory."

But the most famous and most damaging evidence of their own religious motivations appeared in a fund-raising document. In a letter leaked by a mailroom clerk and posted on the Internet in 1999, the Discovery Institute outlined a lengthy twenty-year plan based on Johnson's strategy. The first sentence makes its mission clear: "The proposition that human beings are created in the image of God is one of the bedrock principles on which Western civilization was built."

Known as the Wedge Document, its stated goal is simply "nothing less than the overthrow of materialism and its cultural legacies." It also suggested "possible legal assistance in response to integration of design theory into public school science curricula."

"We are convinced that in order to defeat materialism, we must cut it off at its source. That source is scientific materialism. This is precisely our strategy. If we view the predominant materialistic science as a giant tree, our strategy is intended to function as a 'wedge' that, while relatively small, can split the trunk when applied at its weakest points."

It further states, "Design theory promises to reverse the stifling dominance of the materialist worldview and to replace it with a science consonant with Christian and theistic convictions."

As summer gave way to autumn, the controversy in Dover appeared to have been resolved. Superintendent Nilsen announced that an anonymous donor had purchased sixty copies of *Pandas* to be used for reference material. Members of the public wanted to know where the books came from, but officials wouldn't say. The donor wished to remain anonymous. As Bertha Spahr unpacked the books in her science classroom, she found a pamphlet in the box listing *Pandas* as a textbook about "creation science." But teachers, while not pleased, figured they could store the books in a closet and forget about them. The *York Daily Record* ran an editorial praising an end to the controversy.

Few were prepared for what happened next. On October 18, 2004, Alan Bonsell, as the Dover school board's president, shocked teachers and curriculum advisors when he called for a small but significant change to the ninth-grade biology curriculum.

The board's curriculum committee had been meeting with science teachers and Baksa, the assistant superintendent, for the past several months. The school board had directed the teachers to come up with a change in the biology curriculum that would open the door for discussion about competing theories to evolution. Teachers, trying to accommodate their bosses' concerns, grudgingly accepted the changes. They agreed to say there were problems with the theory of evolution, agreed to acknowledge alternatives, agreed to allow *Pandas* in the classroom, and said they would not teach the origins of life.

But at a meeting in which teachers were not present, committee members Bonsell, Buckingham, and Sheila Harkins added a phrase that included intelligent design.

The teachers finally balked. They removed the phrase. But just before the October 18 school board meeting, the board members reinserted it, presenting it for a vote before the entire board.

As the news of the motion leaked out, a flurry of last-minute e-mails circulated throughout the district, alerting educators and taxpayers as to what was about to take place, urging them to come out to the meeting.

Spahr, as head of the district's science department, could have retired that year with a full pension equal to her salary. Instead, because of the commitment she made to her teachers, she stood at the podium at the meeting and faced the school board members. She begged them not to adopt the policy. She reminded them of past U.S. Supreme Court decisions regarding religion in public school. In a packed room, Buckingham sarcastically asked her, "Where did you get your law degree?"

Neither Nilsen nor Bonsell spoke up to address Buckingham's rudeness to the thirty-year veteran teacher. Spahr pulled back, shocked, and then sat down without saying another word.

Bonsell called a recess in order to meet privately with the other board members.

Before Bonsell could slip into the conference room, Bryan Rehm, the science teacher disgusted by the district's anti-evolution attacks, cornered Bonsell in the hallway. Rehm wanted to know what Bonsell was trying to accomplish. Bonsell told him that man did not come from monkeys. "There are holes in Darwinism so big you can drive a truck through them," Bonsell said.

Bonsell persisted in his motion. Despite pleas from many of the people who filled the cafeteria, the board voted 6–3 to add to the curriculum the sentence "Students will be made aware of the gaps/problems in Darwin's theory and of other theories of evolution, including, but not limited to, intelligent design. Note: Origins of life is not taught."

Board member Casey Brown, who cast one of the three votes opposing the change, quit immediately. She read a resignation letter in which she decried the religious bullying by her fellow board members: "There has been a slow but steady marginalization of some board members. Our opinions are no longer valued or listened to. Our contributions have been minimized or not acknowledged at all. A measure of that is the fact that I myself have been twice asked within the past year if I was 'born again.' No one has, nor should have, the right to ask that of a fellow board member. An individual's religious beliefs should have no impact on his or her ability to serve as a school board director, nor should a person's beliefs be used as a yardstick to measure the value of that service. However, it has become increasingly evident that it is the direction the board has now chosen to go; holding a certain religious belief is of paramount importance."

In tears, Brown said she'd pray for them. Her husband, Jeff, followed his wife's resignation with his own.

Noel Wenrich, who believed in the literal truth of the Bible and spoke of creationism at the June meetings, also voted against the motion. He feared that the curriculum change would lead the district into a costly lawsuit. He said he could have supported the change if the money came from his own wallet. But he believed his fiduciary duty required him to put the wishes of the taxpayers before his own personal religious beliefs. Wenrich was sure the taxpayers didn't want to risk a lawsuit—for any reason. After the meeting, Buckingham and Wenrich shouted at each other in the parking lot. Buckingham called Wenrich an atheist for not supporting him. Wenrich threatened to punch Buckingham.

4

Myth of Separation

Those who expect to reap the blessings of freedom, must, like men, undergo the fatigues of supporting it.

—*Thomas Paine*

The sign outside the Racehorse Tavern says, "God Bless America." The bar sits just outside Dover's dry borders, tucked back off a narrow winding road, surrounded by fields and crumbling foundations of abandoned brick farmhouses. Locals line the cigarette-burned horseshoe bar, playing online poker and talking high school football. The bartender, a surly dark-haired woman, likes to tell demanding customers to fuck themselves. But she's a generous pour to regulars who treat her right. Johnny Cash, a jukebox favorite, sings the truth there.

Steve Stough had been drinking at the Racehorse for more than ten years, sometimes stopping off on the way home from his middle school teaching job in southern York County. Many of the men he used to sit there with are now dead. Today, the bar is lined with new faces. But they've changed little. They still have graying hair and deep creases around their eyes. They work in the factories surrounding York and wear scuffed orange-and-black Harley-Davidson jackets in homage to the motorcycle's local manufacturing plant.

A science teacher and track coach in the Southern York County

School District, Stough wears his white hair cropped close and looks like a drill sergeant. His face is marked by striking contrasts: He has bright blue eyes, a ruddy face, and dazzling white teeth. Stough grew up in West York, a blue-collar borough just south of Dover. He still goes to the local football games. When announcers call out the team roster, Stough recognizes their names as the sons and grandsons of his former classmates.

Stough is a Republican who opposes affirmative action. He attends church most Sundays. He believes in heaven. And he believes in hell. But his hell differs from the Lake of Fire damnation professed by those running Dover's school board. It's like he tells his students about his class: "You have to try to fail."

If you put in the hours and do your homework, he believes, you should have no trouble making it past the Pearly Gates. But Stough had been following what Dover board members were doing and was outraged. As a science teacher, Stough understood that intelligent design could not be a legitimate scientific theory. He had first learned of the concept two years earlier from the head of the science department at his middle school, who warned fellow teachers that it might start worming its way into public debate. Stough knew that the idea of methodological naturalism, on which the rules of science have been firmly grounded since the Enlightenment, limits explanations solely to natural causes. He also knew that intelligent design, with its unnamed designer, relies on the supernatural world to explain how we got here. Stough's daughter, Ashley, was in the eighth grade at Dover's middle school—a year away from taking freshman biology. Stough believes that the idea that "God did it" may belong in Ashley's Sunday school but not in her science class.

Although he spent much of his free time with people at the Racehorse, Stough still felt like an outsider. If he asked the people there, they would probably tell him that God should be taught in public school. Stough, who is uncomfortable with confrontation, knew this and tried to be sensitive to their views.

He wrote an e-mail to his sister in Atlantic City, complaining about what was happening back home. Her reply: "So, what are you going to do about it?" He thought about it for a bit, picked up the phone, and called the American Civil Liberties Union.

Stough wasn't alone. That fall, parents throughout the district faced similar fears and concerns. Following the board's October 18 vote to amend the science curriculum, the ACLU and Americans United for Separation of Church and State began a search for Dover parents interested in suing the district. In newspaper interviews, their lawyers urged residents to contact them. The ACLU set up a special hotline for district residents.

Just as Stough did, other residents sought the opinions of family and friends. Some prayed for guidance. Barrie Callahan, whose persistence brought Bonsell's and Buckingham's creationist agenda out into the open, felt burned out with civic duty since losing her reelection bid a year earlier. But Callahan is proud to consider herself patriotic. She gushes when talking about our Founding Fathers and this nation's principles. She has a mailbox painted red, white, and blue and carries a copy of the Bill of Rights in her purse. She approached the pastor at her Unitarian Church. "Pastor Bob," as Callahan refers to him, told her this attack on evolution was likely part of a national movement led by religious fundamentalists. His words cautioned her. Callahan wasn't interested in tackling a national cause. But neither was she interested in turning her back on what she felt was an important issue in her community. She, too, called the ACLU. Then she told her husband, Fred, that if a lawsuit was filed, she was signing him up as well.

Tammy Kitzmiller's younger daughter, Jess, was already enrolled in Jen Miller's biology class when the board changed the curriculum. She would be one of the first students affected. Tammy Kitzmiller is a reserved single mother of two high school–age girls. She grew up in a fundamentalist Christian family in a tiny town just north of Gettysburg, but she has always been skeptical of organized religion. In Sunday school, she was the problem child. When the teacher told the class that all life was created six thousand years ago and the earth was destroyed by a great flood, Kitzmiller raised her hand. "Then how did Noah fit the dinosaurs on the ark?" she wanted to know. Stough saw intelligent design as an assault on science. Kitzmiller saw it as religion, something only she should be teaching her children.

Still, she was hesitant to take the first step alone. She had only recently moved to the neighborhood and had not yet gotten to know her neighbors. She approached a man who lived across the street and asked him if he was concerned with the new policy. He asked her if she was an atheist.

Kitzmiller also eyed her next-door neighbor Cyndi Sneath. Sneath's boys, Griffin and Nate, were four and seven and played in the tiny creek that stretches along the back of Kitzmiller's property. They track deer footprints that cut into the mud along the bank. Nate is dreamy and likes to draw pictures of trucks. Griffin considers himself an authority on most matters and wants to be an astronaut when he grows up.

Kitzmiller saw Cyndi Sneath outside, smoking a cigarette as her dogs ran around the backyard. Kitzmiller walked up to the rail fence dividing their property. A farmer's open field stretches behind their split-level houses almost to the borough square. When the high school football team plays at home, music from the marching band carries across the field and into their neighborhood. Standing in the long shadows of the late October afternoon, the two women talked about what they feared was happening to their children's education.

The next day, Sneath contacted her state lawmaker, who told her there was little the state could do. In Pennsylvania, local school boards are granted much autonomy. Sneath's only options were to sue the district or vote the board members out of office.

Sneath stewed for the next several days, thinking of little else. She and her husband, Paul, own an appliance repair business in West York, only a few blocks from Alan Bonsell's radiator shop. Going over inventory in the store late one night, Sneath couldn't take it any longer. She picked up the phone at the front counter and called the ACLU. She figured it was too late for someone to be in the office, so she expected to leave a message. That night, Paula Knudsen, an ACLU staff attorney in the Harrisburg office, was working late, sifting through the hotline messages from Dover residents. Some people called to refer someone else. Others called to say they supported what the ACLU was doing but were afraid to come forward themselves. Some said they feared what their neighbors would say, or their families, or the people at their church.

When Knudsen picked up the phone, Sneath expressed her concerns. Knudsen briefly outlined how a lawsuit would work. "Sign me up," Sneath said. She went home and told her husband that she planned to sue the district. Paul just nodded. He supported his wife and agreed with her. But he also knew that when Cyndi's mind was made up, no one could change it. The next day, she approached Kitzmiller. Knudsen had told Sneath that attorneys wanted to talk to parents whose children were already taking biology. Kitzmiller decided to sign up, too.

As Dover parents wrestled with what to do, others farther away got ready. One morning in late October, Eric Rothschild, a thirty-seven-year-old partner in the Philadelphia law firm Pepper Hamilton, sat down at his desk and found he'd received an e-mail from the National Center for Science Education. Eugenie Scott,

NCSE's executive director, who once thought a Dover test case was too good to be true, asked Rothschild if he'd be interested in participating in a possible lawsuit. The ACLU didn't have the resources to pursue it alone. An energetic and tense corporate attorney, Rothschild fired back an e-mail eagerly offering assistance. Rothschild specialized in the complex and technical legal world of reinsurance and commercial litigation. He participated in defending Three Mile Island's insurers in a class-action suit brought against the nuclear power plant's owners. Three Mile Island sits on the Susquehanna River fifteen miles from Dover and less than five miles from where I grew up, in Newberrytown. Following the nuclear power plant's 1979 meltdown, residents claiming to have suffered cancer and other illnesses related to the radiation filed a class-action lawsuit. Rothschild helped dissect the flaws in the scientific claims, and the case was dismissed.

Until he received Scott's e-mail, Rothschild considered his career fairly unremarkable. He possessed a passion for church-and-state issues. Since watching a similar battle play out in Kansas five years earlier, he had dreamed of a First Amendment case for his firm's pro bono division.

As a boy, Rothschild hadn't been particularly interested in science, even though his mother remembers that he possessed an aptitude for the subject. But as a Jew, a member of a religious minority, he was intrigued with what was taking place in Dover. His father's family had fled Germany, arriving in the United States in 1938—just before Kristallnacht and the beginning of the Holocaust. Rothschild understood, if only through his family's heritage, the cost of accepting incremental assaults on civil liberty and religious freedom.

Perhaps more than anything, what appealed to him was that the public's debate over evolution was merely a piece of what was at the heart of the Christian fundamentalist movement.

In the presidential election that year, the Christian right rallied its base on issues of gay marriage, abortion, and public displays of the Ten Commandments. Evolution had been merely a nascent battle in the culture wars, but Rothschild recognized it as one of the issues "swimming about in that pond," as he puts it.

All these conflicts, I believe, stem from the same source. In the evangelical faith, witnessing for the Lord is more than just an expression of one's fervent desire to spread the good news. Converting those who have not yet been washed in the blood of Christ is essential to practicing one's religion. It's a strange twist that in some ways seems to pit the First Amendment's Establishment Clause against its Free Exercise proviso—a demand for tolerance of religious intolerance.

Many of the fundamentalists I've encountered insist, for instance, that the Anti-Defamation League attacks Christians. Why? Because Jewish people are resisting evangelical efforts to convert them. According to 1 John 4:2–3, "Those who do not confess that Jesus Christ has come in the flesh are under the spirit of anti-Christ."

Eugenie Scott referred Rothschild to the Pennsylvania ACLU's legal director, Witold "Vic" Walczak, an amiable, experienced trial attorney based in Pittsburgh on the other side of the state. Walczak had been working with the NCSE for several weeks. Something in his gut told him this was going to be an important case. He had just finished reading *What's the Matter with Kansas*, in which Thomas Frank identified evolution as one of the big religious-right issues.

Like Rothschild, he sensed that Dover, in some way, was connected to what was happening across the country that fall. The evening after Dover's school board adopted intelligent design, Walczak spoke with Eugenie Scott about pursuing a lawsuit.

Walczak possessed a natural empathy for people like Steve

Stough, people who feel set apart from their community. He still remembers the moment he first felt that way himself. In 1964, when Walczak was a toddler, his family had immigrated to the United States from Europe. They settled for a while in Nashville. A Polish-speaking little boy, he had his first American party for his fifth birthday. He invited the children from his kindergarten class. He was allowed to pick whatever kind of cake he wanted, and he asked his father to make him his favorite, a mocha-walnut cake, a dense recipe carried over from Poland.

After everyone sang "Happy Birthday," Walczak happily dug into his cake. But after a few bites, he looked up to see a table of children staring at him. Each of their slices had a fork resting next to it and only one bite missing. In a world of Duncan Hines, this was not proper birthday cake.

Walczak doesn't say that this experience led him to the ACLU. But he remembers it as his first taste of what it was like to not fit in, to be an outsider. For whatever reason, that memory never left him.

Rothschild called Walczak. The two men spoke for twenty minutes.

After he hung up the phone, Rothschild approached his friend and fellow law partner Steve Harvey, a steel-blue–eyed Catholic in his mid-forties with striking white hair. Typically genial and outgoing, Harvey turns into an intimidating interrogator in the courtroom. Tom Schmidt, a staid attorney from Pepper Hamilton's Harrisburg office, also joined the case.

Americans United, which had been monitoring Dover's battle since the June board meetings, wanted to participate. The organization's assistant legal director, Richard Katskee, a First Amendment expert known for his encyclopedic knowledge and the engaging prose he brings to his legal briefs, signed on to the case. Gangly and dark-eyed, Katskee often hides his talent with a self-deprecating demeanor so heavy that it sometimes seems like an act. But his boss, Americans United executive director Barry Lynn, says Katskee's not acting.

Initially, Bryan Rehm, the sharp-tongued physics teacher, wasn't interested in becoming a plaintiff. By November, he had found a job in a neighboring school district. Rather than suing the district, he wanted to join Dover's school board and change the problem from the inside. He applied to fill one of the seats vacated by Jeff and Casey Brown. But during the public interview, Rehm quickly realized that board members had no intention of letting him join. They had already made their choices. Reading printed statements from index cards, Buckingham said, "As a board member, I can practically guarantee that you'll be misquoted and otherwise misrepresented in an effort to keep the public inflamed and sell newspapers. Do you feel able to rise above the constant attacks on the board and to function as a rational board member?"

One by one, the candidates solemnly nodded their heads and acknowledged that it would be difficult, but, yes, they would try. When it was his turn, Rehm responded, "It is a great disservice and fallacy to teach students that a perfectly valid faith constitutes scientific knowledge. It's time to look at these things with a new and fresh perspective that allows for input from all concerned parties. Thank you."

Buckingham listened to Rehm's statement and asked him a question not asked of anyone else: "Have you ever been accused of abusing a child?"

Without flinching, Rehm replied, "I have not."

Even though he teaches science and has extensive experience in curriculum development, Rehm was rejected that night in favor of a man who home schools his children and one who is a Pentecostal minister.

Rehm stands six-foot-five with broad shoulders and heavy-lidded eyes. He is often impatient and unable to sit still. His legs jitter when he tries, the result of what he calls "an undiagnosed motion disorder." He frequently responds to questions with uncomfortable stares and long pauses. He's just composing his thoughts, but to the questioner, it can be terribly intimidating. To his friends and family, he is loyal and dependable. Physically, his wife Christy is strikingly his opposite. An English teacher, she is warm and bubbly with long dark hair. Her husband is angular; she is soft and curvy. She drinks Jameson whiskey. He won't touch coffee.

That summer, Christy gave birth to their fourth child. Their home is chaotic and full of energy and everyone talks at once. For Bryan, church is a much-needed time for quiet spiritual reflection. He and his wife teach summer vacation Bible school. Bryan plays guitar and Christy sings in their church choir. They met as teachers at the local vocational-technology school. Other teachers thought Bryan was odd and ignored him. Christy felt sorry for him.

Bryan grew up just outside of Harrisburg. His mother is a retired schoolteacher. His father worked at the American Can Company. In college, Bryan considered a career as a sound recording engineer. He ran sound for several Christian rock bands.

Christy Rehm grew up in an isolated stretch of the Conewago Hills, born to teenage parents. As a girl, she remembers feeling lonely, cut off from friends. During her senior year at Dover Area High School, she became pregnant. She never married the baby's father. As a single mother, Christy worked her way through college, majoring in English and journalism.

Fifteen years later, Christy still goes to school, now working on a doctorate in educational policy. Today, her oldest daughter, Alix, is a feisty, dark-haired fourteen-year-old with a sharp wit. She goes to school with Alan Bonsell's daughter, Victoria.

That year, Alix and Victoria debated religion and science. Students called Alix "Monkey Girl." But, Alix, who inherited her mother's passion and strength, is quite capable of standing up for herself.

After a school board meeting that fall, Paula Knudsen approached Bryan Rehm. She suggested that he might want to participate in a lawsuit. He and Christy thought about it for a few days and agreed.

Beth Eveland, a paralegal, Girl Scout leader, and mother of two little girls, signed up. She lives across from Harmony Grove Community Church, where Bill Buckingham worships. She didn't believe that Buckingham and Alan Bonsell were motivated by improving science education.

Julie Smith, a single mother and devout Catholic, agreed to join a lawsuit. Her high school daughter, Katherine, was a member of Dover's Bible Club. Joel Leib, an artist and teacher, signed up, along with his common-law wife, Deb Fenimore. Between them, they have five children.

Leib looks like an aging Civil War soldier: He has a droopy mustache and long hair shot with gray that he pulls back in a ponytail. Leib family roots in the area stretch back to the 1600s and the original William Penn land grants. Just outside Dover, in the village of Admire, May's Meeting House stands in an open field. The small brick church bears the brunt of winter winds that sweep down from the northern ridge. There in a tiny graveyard, the area's German-speaking settlers are buried: *"Hier ruhen Henry Leib. Geboren den 26 Feb. 1777. Gestorben den 29 Nov. 1816."*

Today, the meeting house is padlocked, and many of the tombstones have crumbled away. The smell of manure from a nearby dairy hangs heavy in the air. As a young man, Leib gathered acorns from a stand of oaks that tower over the meeting house and stretch their roots into the graves of his ancestors. He soaked the acorns to remove the bitter tannins, and ground them into flour to make bread.

From the beginning, Dover's story caught the attention of a nation bruised red and blue. The national media cast it as a small-town battle of God vs. science, and the school district became a mirror to what was playing out across the country that autumn. Evangelicals, led by patriot pastors and fundamentalist Christian talk radio, celebrated George Bush's victory over John Kerry. With Congress and the executive branch firmly under their control, they eyed the courts as their next great battlefield.

Attorney Richard Thompson told Dover board members they had been chosen to lead the fight. As he was fond of saying, "A revolution in evolution is under way."

In the weeks after the curriculum change, Thompson held conference calls in executive sessions with the Dover board. He discussed legal strategy as board members huddled around the phone, listening to his plans to use Dover to lead the religious revolution. Buckingham remembers Thompson talking dreamily about arguing the case before the U.S. Supreme Court. Thompson boasted he had already started working on his brief.

"I was going to go with him," Buckingham said.

By that fall, I had written several newspaper articles about intelligent design. With little experience in science journalism, I initially tiptoed around the debate of whether there was a legitimate controversy over evolutionary theory. Those with the Discovery Institute, the concept's chief supporter, insisted to me that intelligent design wasn't a religiously based idea. But Bonsell and Buckingham spoke candidly in interviews about their creationist beliefs and why they thought intelligent design was an acceptable compromise between their faith and what the law would allow.

In the weeks leading up to the curriculum change, Bonsell had been especially frank. He explained to me that this nation's founders were Christians who never intended a wall to be erected between government and Protestantism. The First Amendment only applied to other religions, he told me. Bonsell wanted me to come by his garage. He had a copy of David Barton's *Myth of Separation*. He asked me to read it. Then, he promised me, I would understand.

Apparently, I wasn't the only one who had received a copy of the book from Bonsell. The day after the board's curriculum change, a social studies teacher e-mailed Baksa, the assistant superintendent, complaining that Dover had gone from a "standards-driven school district" to a "living-word driven school district." Baksa wrote back, "All kidding aside. Be careful what you ask for." He said Bonsell handed him a copy of Barton's book and that board members were targeting the social studies curriculum next year. "Feel free to borrow my copy to get an idea of where the board is coming from," he wrote.

Bonsell takes the same literalist approach to the U.S. Constitution that he does to the Bible. As both he and Buckingham frequently point out, "Nowhere in the Constitution does it say, 'separation of church and state.'"

And, of course technically, they are correct. It's true. Nowhere in the First Amendment does it say the words "separation of church and state."

The First Amendment states: "Congress shall make no law respecting an establishment of religion, or prohibiting the free exercise thereof . . . ." But as Bonsell explained to me, Barton argues in his book that the First Amendment only refers to the establishment of a specific Protestant denomination. In other words,

Barton claims that Christian founders were saying they couldn't endorse Lutheranism, for instance, over Presbyterianism. But in Barton's view, forcing Christian beliefs on the nation's citizens has always been fair game.

The only problem is that Barton, who had been hired by the Republican National Committee that year to rally the evangelical base, is not the most reliable source. To make his case, he cites quotations of the Founding Fathers that are either questionable or outright false.[1] Additionally, there is ample historical evidence that a wall of separation between church and government was precisely what the founders had in mind when they wrote the First Amendment. Thomas Jefferson and Benjamin Franklin were deists, believing the world had been created in the past but that the creator was no longer involved in its day-to-day operations.

The word "God" appears nowhere in the Constitution. The Treaty of Tripoli, read before then-president John Adams on the Senate floor in 1798, specifically states, "As the government of the United States of America is not, in any sense, founded on the Christian Religion . . . ."

As for the actual words "separation of church and state," the reference comes from an 1802 letter Jefferson wrote to members of the Danbury Baptist Association. The Connecticut Baptists had been seeking clarification of the First Amendment's intent as it related to religious freedom. In response, Jefferson wrote,

> Believing with you that religion is a matter which lies solely between man & his god, that he owes account to none other for his faith or his worship, that the legitimate powers of government reach actions only, and not opinions, I contemplate with sovereign reverence that act of the whole American people which declared that their legislature should make no law respecting an establishment of religion, or prohibiting the free

exercise thereof, thus building a wall of separation between church and state.

In early December, the administration issued a news release that accused the press of misreporting the facts. Despite published accounts, the release said, Dover would not be "teaching intelligent design." Rather, the district would merely be "making students aware" of the concept. It also included the four-paragraph statement that would be read to students in January:

> The Pennsylvania Academic Standards require students to learn about Darwin's Theory of Evolution and eventually to take a standardized test of which evolution is a part.
>
> Because Darwin's Theory is a theory, it continues to be tested as new evidence is discovered. The theory is not a fact. Gaps in the theory exist for which there is no evidence. A theory is defined as a well-tested explanation that unifies a broad range of observations.
>
> Intelligent Design is an explanation of the origin of life that differs from Darwin's view. The reference book *Of Pandas and People* is available in the library along with other resources for students who might be interested in gaining an understanding of what Intelligent Design actually involves.
>
> With respect to any theory, students are encouraged to keep an open mind. The school leaves the discussion of the Origins of Life to individual students and their families. As a Standards-driven district, class instruction focuses upon preparing students to achieve proficiency on Standards-based assessments.

The Discovery Institute, intelligent design's nerve center, understood what was at stake. In a news release of its own, it announced its opposition to the statement.

Just as those with the National Center for Science Education knew the risks inherent in embarking on the wrong test case, so did those at Discovery. If the courts determined intelligent design was merely revamped creationism, it could destroy their entire movement.

With the lawsuit imminent, Discovery endorsed a biology curriculum that takes a "teach the controversy" approach or "critical analysis" of evolution, rather than one that incorporates intelligent design. The organization employed a similar tactic in Ohio two years earlier as the state was revamping its science standards. At first, the organization pushed for intelligent design in Ohio's science curriculum, but switched to embracing a "teach the controversy" curriculum amid threats of lawsuits.[2]

That fall, Seth Cooper, a Discovery Institute attorney, flew to Pennsylvania and met privately with Dover's board members in Salem Elementary School's conference room. Cooper stared at the board members who enthusiastically wanted to help the Discovery Institute fulfill its mission. He urged them to drop the curriculum change. Convinced they were doing the right thing, board members ignored the advice and pressed on.

After the presidential election, journalists from around the world started calling on Dover. BBC news crews came to Pennsylvania and asked pointed questions. Europe, fascinated by this nation's support of George Bush, sent reporters who searched for insight into the U.S. evangelical movement and its devoted political following. A British news crew tagged along with the Rehms to Bryan's parents' house for Thanksgiving dinner.

In contemporary shorthand describing America's cultural divide, Pennsylvania is a "Blue state," owing its sliver of a Democratic majority to its two major cities. (James Carville famously described the state as Philadelphia and Pittsburgh with Alabama in between.) The rest, especially York County, is a GOP haven.

But York County's Republican roots are surprisingly shallow. Throughout most of the twentieth century, the Democratic Party held the majority, due largely to the historical antifederalist alignment of local Pennsylvania Germans. Dover was part of what was known as the county's Black Belt—areas so steadfastly Democratic that Republican Party officials wouldn't bother to venture there with registration petitions.

But with the 1960 presidential election battle between John F. Kennedy and Richard Nixon, the political tide began to drift right. Nixon, due to strong local connections, was a popular candidate. His parents lived for a time on a farm outside of York, and Nixon's brother graduated from a high school just outside of Dover. Anti-Catholic sentiments among York County Protestants fueled antipathy toward Kennedy.[3]

Republican inroads made in 1960 flourished over the next two decades. Despite their heritage, York County voters more closely identified with conservative issues. Steve Nickol, a state lawmaker whose own York County roots stretch back to before the Revolutionary War, calls it the "grim reaper" effect. As stalwart Democrats died out, they were replaced by new registrations of voting-age Republicans. In the mid-1980s, the county finally flipped to a GOP majority.

On December 20, the plaintiffs' attorneys announced the filing of *Kitzmiller v. Dover* from beneath the ornate gold dome of Pennsylvania's Capitol in Harrisburg. The school board and its legal team may have seen Dover as part of this nation's culture war, but the parents viewed it as an issue critical to their town. They were shocked by the turnout of the national media at the press conference.

Though Dover is a small community, most of the eleven parents named in the lawsuit had never met. Still strangers, they huddled together, leaning on each other for support as they balanced precariously on metal risers. Over their heads, circling the ceiling of the rotunda, were the inscribed words of Pennsylvania's Quaker founder, William Penn: "There may be room there for such a holy experiment, for the nations want a precedent. And my God will make it the seed of a nation. That an example may be set up to the nations. That we may do the thing that is truly wise and just."

Television crews stepped around the parents, setting up cameras and microphones. Tammy Kitzmiller, Christy Rehm, Cyndi Sneath, and Beth Eveland stared at the chairs, which quickly filled up with reporters. Facing the grand marble staircase leading to the legislative chambers, they wondered whether they had made the right decision.

Rothschild stepped nervously into the spotlight and said that the lawsuit wasn't an attack on religion. No, he pointed out, many of the plaintiffs held strong religious views and were regular churchgoers. Because her daughter was already taking biology and would be among the first to be read the four-paragraph statement, Kitzmiller had become the lead plaintiff. Terrified, she waited her turn to speak. She had never spoken in public before. Her voice trembled slightly as she addressed the cameras and said she believed that teaching her daughters about religion was her right and not the privilege of the school board. As she spoke, a man in a fur hat and his wife, wearing a handkerchief covering her hair, sneaked up behind the plaintiffs. They waved fluorescent green signs for the cameras that said, "ACLU Censors Truth."

The couple pushed closer to the parents, scaring the already frightened women until their attorney, Steve Harvey, chased the interlopers away. Later, the anti-ACLU couple pressed literature into my hand written by creationist Kent "Dr. Dino" Hovind.

The pamphlets claimed that dinosaurs and man walked the earth together.

That evening Judge John E. Jones III, driving home to Pottsville, listened to the local news and caught a report on the press conference. Intrigued by the mention of intelligent design, he wondered on whose judicial docket the civil case would appear.

That December, Dover became consumed by the battle over intelligent design. Each year, Bertha Spahr, the tough-demeanored head of the science department, baked chocolate-dipped biscotti for her teachers. Distracted by the fight, she said there was too little time and even less holiday spirit. Next year, she promised.

Steve Stough felt sick to his stomach when he thought of attending the first school board meeting following the press conference. He read of the fight that almost took place between Buckingham and Wenrich in the parking lot and feared a confrontation. But Stough was determined not to be cowed into staying away. Before he left for the meeting, he stepped into his bathroom and threw up.

He and his wife Susan pulled into the elementary school parking lot, trying to ignore the cars bearing "I support Dover School Board" bumper stickers. Christmas was only a week away. As board members formally announced they had hired the Thomas More Law Center to represent the district, the Stoughs hunched on metal chairs, scrawling their names on Christmas cards and licking envelopes.

Bryan Rehm, meanwhile, stood at the front of the room with a video camera. Perhaps sensing what board members were planning, he had asked for audiotapes of the June board meetings. Officials told him the tapes had been destroyed. Rehm began videotaping the meetings, an imposing figure staring at board members through a lens.

The board appointed Sheila Harkins its new president. In her first order of business, she changed the rules of public comment. People were permitted to address only issues already on the board's meeting agenda. When citizens tried to talk about intelligent design, which was never on the agenda, Harkins banged her gavel and told them they were out of order.

As Rehm watched and the Stoughs signed cards, a *Nightline* producer and a camera crew filmed from the back of the room. Later, a producer asked Harkins to explain intelligent design. A bubbly blond with a grown daughter, Harkins tried to dodge the question. She handed him an e-mail from a supporter. He shook his head. He wanted to hear her explain it.

Backing through a door, she stammered. Finally, haltingly, she offered, "It's exploring the scientific theories of it. Is that what you're saying? . . . [The e-mail says] to teach the children the scientific diversities. Is that what you're asking?" She ducked behind a door and disappeared.

One person was noticeably absent from December's meeting. Bonsell said he had heard that Buckingham was visiting family. Board members said they thought he was in California. Then, Alabama.

Buckingham was still struggling with his OxyContin addiction and had checked himself back into a rehabilitation treatment center.

Meanwhile, the media swarmed the parents. Kitzmiller told her daughters not to answer the phone. She had gone home at the end of the day and eyed the blinking light on her answering machine. Consumed by the case, the plaintiffs seldom talked of anything but creationism and intelligent design and evolutionary theory. Finally their family members could no longer listen and turned away. But they couldn't stop, and so they turned to each other. Stough suggested that they meet at the Racehorse

Tavern. It quickly became their place for discussing strategy and exchanging information. Stough called it their security blanket, a shelter hidden down a back road. Far from the storm of controversy, they played pool and talked about what was happening to their lives and wondered together what awaited them in the new year.

5

"Never Said It"

Thou shall not bear false witness against thy neighbor.
— *Exodus 20:16*

As Dover slipped into a new year, Dover's attorney, Richard Thompson, faced a dilemma. The trial was still months away, but in two days, his clients would be asked to recount the remarks they had made about teaching creationism alongside evolution.

It was, for Thompson, certainly a problem. In a couple of weeks, teachers were to tell students about intelligent design. Though school officials argued they were only making students "aware" of the concept, the truth was that for the first time in the country, intelligent design would be taught as a required part of a public school science curriculum. The statement contained only four short and seemingly innocuous paragraphs, but Thompson intended to use it as a wedge for something much bigger. It was the camel's nose nudged under the tent, "a modest proposal" designed to squeak past church-and-state challenges.

But in order to succeed, Thompson needed to convince the judge that board members were merely interested in improving science education.

And that was why he had a dilemma.

Parents' attorneys intended to halt the district before students heard the statement. In a court motion, they requested the right to seek a temporary restraining order. As part of the discovery process, they scheduled depositions for January 3. Attorneys sought to get board members' published creationist remarks into the court record to establish their religious motivations behind the biology curriculum change. If the attorneys were successful, they could extinguish Thompson's revolutionary spark before it became a flame.

Board members, especially Bonsell and Buckingham, had made it clear in public discussions that their true concern with the biology curriculum was based on their belief that evolution contradicts a literal reading of the Bible. Fortunately, and conveniently for their case, recordings from the meetings in which they had spoken of creationism had been erased. But newspaper articles about the meetings remained.

It was definitely a problem. But here's the thing: What if Bonsell, Buckingham, and other board members hadn't said it? What if they hadn't been talking about creationism but instead had been discussing intelligent design all along?

The problem would no longer exist.

Whether Thompson ultimately solved this problem for himself or it was the inspiration of his clients remains one of the case's unanswered questions.

I have spent countless hours trying to figure out why Dover officials chose to do what they did that day. For me, it's the most vexing part of the story: Who made the decision to lie?

Of course, the resolution of Thompson's dilemma led to a series of dilemmas for others. The parents' attorneys, the students sitting in the classroom, me—all of us were forced to grapple with the consequences of board members' faulty memories and outright denials. The most painful dilemma wouldn't be apparent for months, however, when two earnest, hardworking reporters would be forced to choose between a judge's order and the possibility of going to jail. But that would come later.

★ ★ ★

The parents' attorneys Rothschild and Harvey drove from Harrisburg to Dover that morning, chatting about what they expected would play out in the day's depositions. They felt prepared, so they weren't overly concerned. The day started amiably enough. Their colleagues in the case, the ACLU's Vic Walczak and Americans United's Richard Katskee, met them at Dover's administration building. The four men planned to question Buckingham, Bonsell, Sheila Harkins, who was now the school board's president, and Superintendent Nilsen. Thompson and another Thomas More attorney, Patrick Gillen, had already arrived in town. For several hours the previous evening, they had met with Dover officials, poring over details of the case.

When the parents' attorneys look back on what they tried to accomplish that day, they agree that they'd thought it would be a slam-dunk. Even Rothschild, who is often cautious in recounting key trial events, admits this. Attorneys merely wanted to confirm board members' creationist remarks made six months earlier at June's public meetings—remarks made before a crowd of about a hundred people and reported by the two local newspapers. Judge Jones would rely on precedent established by the U.S. Supreme Court's *Lemon v. Kurtzman* decision, which details the requirements for legislation concerning religion. Jones would review the material facts of the case—the creationist remarks—and realize that the board's primary purpose had been to advance religion. He'd grant the temporary restraining order. Board members, realizing that they had embarked on a misguided cause, would withdraw the curriculum change and agree not to force intelligent design in science class.

That was supposed to be the way it worked, anyway.

Harvey, with Katskee providing backup, interviewed Harkins

as Thompson monitored the questions. A Quaker, Harkins affirmed she would answer all questions truthfully. But an odd thing happened only minutes into her deposition. In her testimony, she contradicted the reporters' accounts. At Harvey's questioning, Harkins said flatly, "We never looked for a book that included both creationism and evolution, never."

Harvey remembers being a bit startled, but pressed on in his questioning. He asked her about Buckingham's remark, "Two thousand years ago, someone died on the cross. Won't someone stand up for him?"

Cheerfully, Harkins said Buckingham made the remark, but not in June. Rather, she said, it was said at an October 2003 board meeting during a debate supporting the phrase, "Under God," in the Pledge of Allegiance.

"He never said that again," she told Harvey.

A similar scene took place in another building at the same time. Rothschild was going through a testy exchange with the superintendent, as Gillen and Walczak looked on. Richard Nilsen has a narrow face and a bushy mustache and looks a lot like the cartoon character Ned Flanders from *The Simpsons*. But he lacks Flanders's upbeat expressions such as "okaly dokaly." Instead, Nilson speaks in a terse monotone.

In account after account, Nilsen denied hearing creationism discussed at the June meetings.

"Do you remember Mr. Buckingham making any statements about the curriculum committee looking for a book that presented both creationism and evolution?" Rothschild asked.

"I don't remember that, no," Nilsen said.

"Do you remember him making statements like that at any time?"

"No."

"Do you remember Mr. Buckingham ever bringing up the

subject of creationism at any school board meeting?" Rothschild asked.

"Not that I can remember."

"Do you remember any other school board member bringing up the subject of creationism at any school board meeting?" Rothschild said, trying one more time.

"Not that I can remember," Nilsen repeated.

Rothschild kept firing questions, and the superintendent kept saying he didn't remember.

Exasperated, Rothschild finally said, "Mr. Nilsen, do I understand you correctly that not withstanding the fact that there are many articles during this June period about discussion about teaching creationism, you have no recollection of the subject of creationism at any school board meeting?"

"That's correct," Nilsen said.

In both rooms, attorneys were dumbfounded. Astounded by Nilsen's version of events, Rothschild and Walczak finished the deposition and searched for their colleagues. Harvey and Katskee, equally shocked, looked for them.

When the four men caught up to each other, they stumbled over each other's sentences, rushing to spill the news: "You won't believe what happened."

As the attorneys compared notes, they agreed it was terribly strange that Nilsen's and Harkins' statements contradicted the newspaper articles. They considered the possibility that the newspaper accounts were inaccurate. Wary and skeptical, the attorneys resumed the depositions that afternoon.

From the start, Rothschild found himself frustrated with each sentence Bonsell uttered. A deposition typically serves as an efficient, straightforward method for establishing the facts. As long as those questioned are willing to tell the truth, that is. While the person deposed typically doesn't volunteer information cheerfully, Rothschild rarely finds himself confronting outright lies. When he thinks back on it, Rothschild occasionally wonders whether it's possible that Bonsell had convinced himself that what he said was true.

Bonsell repeated each question, forcing Rothschild to ask it again. He feigned confusion. He'd stop and say he was only trying to understand. But even with a casual reading of the transcripts, it's apparent. Underneath Bonsell's innocent demeanor, there was an obvious contempt for the process.

In one lengthy exchange, as he tried to get Bonsell to differentiate between teaching students about intelligent design and the district's assertion that it was merely making them aware of the concept, Rothschild began to lose patience:

"Why do you say you are not requiring the teaching?" he asked.

"That is exactly what it says in our release. We are not teaching it," Bonsell said.

"What do you understand the school teachers will be doing in class as a result of the change in the biology curriculum?" Rothschild asked.

"They will be doing exactly what it says in here. They will be reading a statement to them," Bonsell said.

"And in your view, is reading that statement teaching or not teaching?" Rothschild asked.

"No. It is not teaching," Bonsell said.

"When the students hear that statement, will they be learning?" Rothschild asked.

"They will be being made aware of," Bonsell said.

"Will they be learning, Mr. Bonsell?" Rothschild asked.

Thompson, at this point, interjected. "He has answered the question. Asked and answered," he said.

"You may answer the question," Rothschild told Bonsell.

"They will be made aware of," Bonsell said.

"Will they be learning or not learning, Mr. Bonsell?" Rothschild asked.

Thompson again interjected. "Objection, asked and answered. You are getting argumentative. You have asked the same question over and over again," he said.

"I have not. I am asking for an answer to my question," Rothschild said.

"He just said [they] would be aware of is what he means it is, and it is not teaching," Thompson said.

"In your view, Mr. Bonsell, as a member of the school board, when the students hear the statement that you are requiring teachers to read, will they be learning or not learning?" Rothschild continued.

"In what context do you mean?" Bonsell asked.

"Mr. Bonsell, did you go to school?" Rothschild asked.

"Did I go to school?" Bonsell asked.

"Yes," Rothschild said.

"Yes," Bonsell said.

"Is that a yes?" Rothschild asked.

"Yes," Bonsell said.

"Did you learn in school?" Rothschild asked.

"Yes," Bonsell said.

"Do you understand what the word 'learn' means?" Rothschild asked.

"To be taught, to teach. That is why I am saying. I need to know what your definition of that is because I am not going to get caught in these . . ." Bonsell said.

"I am going to ask you the same question. If you are not able to answer, please tell me. When the students hear the statement that you are requiring school teachers to read, will they be learning?" Rothschild asked.

"Asked and answered," Thompson said. "Objection. Asked and answered several times now."

"So what do we do?" Bonsell asked.

"He has objected," Rothschild said.

"I have objected," Thompson said. "He has answered the question. He said it is not learning. It is making aware of. You don't like his answer, but you can't keep on asking the same question."

"He didn't say it was not learning," Rothschild said to Thompson.

"It is not learning," Thompson said.

"Is that your answer?" Rothschild asked Bonsell.

"If learning is teaching, no," Bonsell said.

"I want a yes or no. Are they learning or not learning?" Rothschild said.

"Like what I just said, if your definition of learning is teaching, then no," Bonsell said.

"Nobody's definition of learning is teaching," Rothschild said, clearly frustrated.

Later, Rothschild brought up the issue of the June board meetings. He asked Bonsell to look at a June 15, 2004, article written for the *York Dispatch* by Heidi Bernhard-Bubb.

Rothschild then asked, "Is Ms. Bernhard-Bubb another one of these reporters who gets stuff wrong about the biology curriculum issue?"

"Yes," Bonsell said.

"At the very beginning of her article, it says nearly a hundred Dover residents and teachers attended last night's school board meeting to continue debating whether creationism should be taught alongside evolution in the high school's biology curriculum. Does this article accurately report that creationism was being debated at school board meetings?" Rothschild asked.

"Absolutely not," Bonsell said.

"There was no discussion about creationism?" Rothschild asked.

"No," Bonsell said.

"So as we look through these articles—this uninterrupted series of articles about June meetings that talk about creationism being debated at the school board meetings and statements made by school board members, including yourself, about creationism, all of those are just fabricated?" Rothschild asked.

"Fabricated?" Bonsell asked.

"Yes, fabricated," Rothschild said.

"Fabricated? You mean she just made them all up, is that what you mean?" Bonsell asked.

"There's a lot of statements in here about people talking about creationism. I think you are suggesting to me it never happened," Rothschild said.

"All this debate about creationism, yes, that never did happen. It was not a debate about creationism," Bonsell said.

Meanwhile, as Rothschild grew more irritated, Harvey wrestled with similar emotions as he questioned Buckingham. A few days earlier, the board member completed a twenty-eight-day drug rehabilitation program for his OxyContin addiction at a facility in Allentown—his second time in rehab that year.

But to the lawyers, Buckingham didn't appear overly shaken, or fragile, as one might expect from someone fresh out of drug treatment. When he admitted that he didn't know if the painkiller had damaged his recollection of events, he made a joke about his wife thinking he might have a bad memory.

Still, Buckingham's version of events echoed the accounts of Nilsen and Harkins and Bonsell. He adamantly denied making any remarks about creationism. He said no one else had mentioned creationism either.

Harvey asked him about his published statement that he wants a book that offers a balance between the Christian view of creationism and evolution.

"Never said it," Buckingham said.

As for his remark "This country wasn't founded on Muslim beliefs or evolution, this country was founded on Christianity," Buckingham said, "I never said that."

"You never said that at all?" Harvey asked.

"Not to my knowledge," Buckingham said.

Finally, Harvey stopped asking questions about the June meetings. "Mr. Buckingham, I don't mean to get into your personal issues again, but I think I need to ask this question as well, and that there is a pretty big disconnect in this case between what the newspapers are saying and what the witnesses that we've talked to today are saying to us, especially you," Harvey said. "You did have some drug issue in your recent past or somewhat recent past. Is it your understanding that that would in any way affect your memory or ability to remember these things?"

"I didn't understand that, but OxyContin is a relatively new drug, and the long-term effects of it aren't known, so I don't know. They could well be. I don't know," Buckingham said.

"Are you taking anything like cold medicine or anything today that would affect your ability to remember the events correctly?" Harvey asked.

Buckingham responded, "No. I have a Hall's right now."

Despite his amiable demeanor, Buckingham still blamed the local newspapers for getting their facts wrong. He said that, beyond the obituaries and the sports page, he no longer read the papers.

During the depositions, it became obvious that board members did almost no homework in preparation. They were hopelessly, willfully ignorant of the most basic principles of science and could not produce a rudimentary definition of intelligent design.

When pressed, Buckingham provided a definition for intelligent design that more closely resembled evolutionary theory.

"Scientists, a lot of scientists—don't ask me the names. I can't tell you where it came from," he said. "A lot of scientists believe that back through time, something, molecules, amoeba, whatever, evolved into the complexities of life we have now."

Bonsell, at first, could only say intelligent design "is a scientific theory that differs from Darwin's theory."

"How does it differ from Darwin's theory?" Rothschild asked.

"How does it differ?" Bonsell asked. "From what I have read and from the scientists that I have read about, basically Darwin—I mean this is very generalized. But Darwin said everything basically happened by chance. Where intelligent design says that it didn't happen that way. It was the opposite theory."

"How did it happen if it didn't happen by chance?" Rothschild asked.

"I can't answer that," Bonsell said.

When asked, Harkins said the *Pandas* textbook was about intelligent design.

Anything else other than intelligent design that it covered?

"Oh, it had lots of things in it," she told Harvey.

"I'm just asking if you can remember anything that was covered in there," he asked.

"Oh, I remember some flowers," she said, "something about flowers in there."

Board members spoke of taking their case all the way to the U.S. Supreme Court, but they lacked the commitment to understand what they were fighting for. They wanted it taught to children, but were too lazy to learn about it for themselves.

The hubris of the Dover officials was stunning. Many amazing and dramatic moments related to the case would take place in the next year, both inside and outside the courtroom, both in Dover and across the country. But if not for the board members' disavowal of their remarks that day, it's likely none of those moments would have followed. The world would have forgotten about Dover, and Thompson would have had to search for another test case.

The four plaintiffs' attorneys recognized that board members were lying, but they had little time for outrage. Rather, they now faced a dilemma. Their deadline to file an injunction was in less than forty-eight hours. But with the facts of the case now in dispute, they disagreed over what should be done. Should they pursue their request for a temporary restraining order? Or should they allow students to hear the statement and fight it out later in the courtroom?

The attorneys gathered at a Harrisburg bar and argued.

Walczak was usually a huge fan of the temporary restraining order. Among his peers, he was known as "Mr. TRO." He has been told that in his fourteen years with the ACLU, he has successfully sought more restraining orders than any other ACLU attorney in the country. But in this case, he was reluctant.

A failure could predispose the judge to a view he might hold even through the trial. Katskee and Walczak feared that pursuit of a restraining order would be rash and could jeopardize the entire case. They argued in favor of being pragmatic, taking the position that this was about more than just the eleven parents. If they lost, intelligent design would likely spread to other schools.

But Rothschild and Harvey believed they still had a reasonable shot at an injunction. As corporate attorneys, they were fiercely loyal to their new clients. They argued passionately about their obligation to Tammy Kitzmiller's daughter Jess, who would be in the classroom when the statement was read.

The attorneys were still getting to know each other. This would be their first test of how well they would work together. Walczak and Katskee listened to the corporate attorneys and feared they might be dealing with cowboys.

The debate continued late that night and stretched out into a conference call the next day. Finally, they reached an agreement. Rothschild picked up the phone and called Kitzmiller. He told her he was sorry. They wouldn't be seeking an injunction. As Rothschild struggled to apologize, Kitzmiller remembered how upset he sounded and tried to reassure him he had not let her down.

But now, Kitzmiller's daughter had a dilemma. As one of the 150 students taking biology class at Dover that semester, Jess Kitzmiller wasn't happy with the statement that would soon be read to her.

The fourteen-year-old was going to have to decide whether to sit quietly in class and listen to the remarks, or risk ridicule by stepping out into the hall in protest. She talked to her mother and sixteen-year-old sister, Megan, about what to do. They told her it was up to her, and they would support her either way.

As Jess wrestled with what to do, the science teachers also faced a dilemma.

Miller and Eshbach and the rest of the science faculty didn't feel they could in good conscience read the statement to their students. Although they feared for their jobs, they were nonetheless unwilling to compromise. They sat down over lunch with Spahr and their state union representative and crafted a letter. Citing their ethical obligation and solemn responsibility to the truth, they wrote that they could not knowingly give out information to students that they knew to be false:

"Intelligent design is not science. Intelligent design is not biology. Intelligent design is not an accepted scientific theory.

"I believe that if I as the classroom teacher read the required statement, my students will inevitably (and understandably) believe that Intelligent Design is a valid scientific theory, perhaps on par with the theory of evolution. That is not true. To refer the students to *Of Pandas and People* as if it is a scientific resource breaches my ethical obligation to provide them with scientific knowledge that is supported by recognized scientific proof or theory."

Thompson, who touts the importance of academic freedom, immediately blasted the teachers' decision, adding "The Dover faculty have no right to opt out of a legal directive." Nonetheless, with the statement only days away from being read, officials came up with a compromise. Superintendent Nilsen and Assistant Superintendent Baksa stepped in and said they would read the statement to students.

Two days after the plaintiffs' decision not to seek an injunction, Nilsen sent out his weekly memo to the school board. "As you are by now aware, the time and effort put in over the holidays has produced a positive impact. The plaintiffs, ACLU, could not find anything to file an injunction on our biology curriculum. In conjunction with the Thomas More lawyers, Mr. Baksa, Mr. Buckingham, Mr. Bonsell, and Mrs. Harkins did a great job. The ACLU is doing a great job of putting a 'positive spin' on the situation, but I cannot help but feel gratified that they could not stop the implementation, and you know if they could, they would have."

The night of the depositions, Steve Harvey called me as I was getting ready to leave work. Harvey works hard to keep his voice at an even tempo. In court, he writes across the top of documents the reminder, "Slow down."

But on this night, his frustration was audible. He talked so fast I could barely understand him. He told me board members denied ever using the word "creationism." They said the newspaper reporters lied.

This was so absurd to me that I couldn't grasp what he was say-ing, and he had to keep repeating it. I'm not sure who it was, but one of the lawyers in the background, probably exasperated by my obtuseness, said something like, "They called you liars, Lauri."

I sat at my desk with my mouth hanging open. How could they do such a thing? What about the Lord's commandment about not bearing false witness?

I had been talking to Bonsell and Buckingham for months and they had never mentioned that their religious remarks had been misquoted. To the contrary, they talked at length about their per-sonal belief in creationism. The only discrepancy that Bonsell had brought to my attention was to point out that the media shouldn't be writing that the district was "teaching" intelligent design, be-cause it was merely "making students aware" of the concept. And even though I thought that was a ridiculous distinction, I changed the wording in my stories to reflect their position. But in the six months since the June board meetings, Bonsell never said to me, or Maldonado, or any editors at the *York Daily Record* that they had never talked about creationism.

I only hope Dover's officials didn't realize what they had done to Maldonado and Bernhard-Bubb. They callously denounced their journalistic integrity. So, what was I supposed to do? Many people, including colleagues, believe journalistic objectivity de-mands that reporters treat both sides equally and leave the context to the editorial page.

So, according to those rules, I was now in an awkward posi-tion. By using that approach, I had to balance the reality that board members had lied with the notion that two reporters from separate newspapers, both of whom I had worked with before and knew as honest, might have colluded to report that board mem-bers said something that they didn't—and that no one had both-ered to say anything about it for six months.

I thought about the local attention of the June meetings and figured, perhaps, one of the area television stations might have covered it. When I reached Jenn Sherlock, a reporter with the local Fox News television station, she told me that she had indeed interviewed Bill Buckingham on the night of the second June meeting.

"Did he mention creationism?" I asked.

"Oh sure," she told me.

"Creationism, not intelligent design," I asked.

"Creationism," she said. On this point, she was emphatic.

"Can I see the tape?" I asked.

"Sure, come on over," she said.

Minutes later, I stood in the TV station's basement holding my breath as a producer cued up the tape. Wearing sunglasses and his signature American flag lapel pin, Buckingham looked at the camera and said, "We're just looking for a textbook that balances the teaching of evolution with something else, like creationism."

Excited, I jumped up and down as Sherlock and the producer laughed at me. But I didn't care. I now had a story that didn't just parrot the two sides. I could write the truth.

After the struggles that so many people had endured to get to this point, the day the statement was read turned out to be anticlimactic. Nilsen and Baksa took turns in the biology classes. As they entered, teachers gathered students who chose not to participate and stepped out into the hallway.

Jess Kitzmiller reached her decision the night before. She joined her teacher Jen Miller, along with a handful of other students. As the administrator read the printed statement, Kitzmiller waited outside staring wordlessly at the others. The students who remained in the classroom were not allowed to ask questions. The entire affair was all over in about a minute.

Meanwhile, outside Dover High School, the media gathered. Because school officials refused to let journalists on district property, reporters huddled on the sidewalk in the cold, and camera crews waited in heated vans across the street. When school let out, we flocked around students as they made their way to buses and cars, pressing microphones into their faces and eliciting responses for our notebooks.

But few students had anything interesting to say. Most of the ones I spoke with that day said they didn't really care much either way about the statement. I struggled to coax some insight out of one boy who had been in the class, but he only shrugged his shoulders. "I wasn't really paying attention."

Another student told me that he found all the hoopla "kinda dumb."

The most intriguing remarks came from a group of students hanging out in the parking lot of the pizza shop across the street, smoking cigarettes. One girl suggested that if they want to teach intelligent design, perhaps they should also be teaching Rastafarianism, complete with its religious rituals of marijuana use. Her friends high-fived her and all agreed, "Dude!"

Perhaps students might have paid closer attention if they had understood that this was about more than four simple paragraphs. Next Thompson put out a press release under a headline addressing his recurring theme, "A Revolution in Evolution is Underway."

"The small town of Dover, Pennsylvania today became the first school district in the nation to officially inform students of the theory of intelligent design, as an alternative to Darwin's theory of evolution. In what has been called a 'measured step,' 9th grade biology students in the Dover Area School District were read a four-paragraph statement Tuesday morning explaining that Darwin's theory is not a fact and continues to be tested. The statement continued, 'Intelligent design is an explanation of the origin of life that differs from Darwin's view.' "

Thompson told the Associated Press, "This is the first step. . . ."

6

Kidnapped by Baptists

It is those who know little, and not those who know much, who so positively assert that this or that problem will never be solved by science.

—*Charles Darwin, The Descent of Man*

Dover's Conewago Hills are where you can still find hogmaw, a traditional Pennsylvania Dutch dish of stuffed pig's stomach, at Sunday church suppers. Where, in tongue-speaking revivals, people testify to going further with God and to have been shaken over the mouths of hell, not once, not twice, but three times. Where, in a church of whitewashed cinder blocks, a woman said that, yes, God saved her mother before taking her, and where, the woman is promised, he will yet save her children.

It is where, in May, the winding back-country roads are lined with redbud trees bursting with impossibly pink blooms, where calves romp and butt heads in bursts of unbridled giddiness, unable to understand spring's renewal without the experience of the long wait of winter. Still, they know, or sense, and so they play.

But it is also where on dark October nights, dried corn stalks shiver and rattle in the wind that sweeps down into the valleys and where fog pools and swirls in the hollows. It is where, in 1972, Klansmen burned crosses at the Susquehanna Speedway, the local racetrack, sending sparks into the darkened sky over Bald Hill, and where, under a Christian cross, the stained glass window of a local church today still bears the words "donated by Carfield Klan. KKK."

Dover is like every small town. It has stories of startling beauty and secrets of profound ugliness.

In the weeks leading up to spring, school board members no longer publicly discussed intelligent design. But their attacks on the media became more personal. I sat next to Joe Maldonado when Sheila Harkins, in front of a crowded room, said that he intentionally lied in his newspaper articles. She announced that he fabricated a controversy in order to raise money for his son's college tuition.

Those in the room groaned. I watched Maldonado and held my breath. He earns $52.50 a story—and an extra $5 if the story makes it onto the front page. Because he's a reporter, and not supposed to be drawn into the story, Maldonado accepted the woman's remarks, offering not a word of defense. Instead, he kept his head down and scribbled in his notebook, silently overcoming his anger by counting to one hundred. Only the tips of his ears, burning bright red, gave away his feelings.

This incident makes me think that on some level, the board members, at least those who slandered Maldonado so publicly, had convinced themselves they were telling the truth. Or perhaps they knew they lied, and at first, it had been impersonal. They simply jumped on the blame-the-media bandwagon. Only afterwards did they realize that their accusations meant they were impugning the integrity of this man who sat in front of them twice a month, chatting with them after meetings, who had all their home phone numbers and spoke with them frequently, who lived in their community and attended their churches.

There was nothing impersonal about it.

Although Maldonado shared his Christian faith with them,

they demonized him—at least in their own minds. How else could they sleep at night?

Maldonado home schools his younger son, Jaryid, and belongs to the York County Homeschool Association, an organization made up largely of devout Christians. Its members sent e-mails to each other, e-mails that found their way into Maldonado's inbox. They wrote of Dover's battle and accused the media of lying about board member's religious remarks. The writers asked everyone on the list to pray for Dover's school board.

Maldonado and I have had long conversations at his sandwich stand. I've told him I'm angry at Christians who have placed him in this position. He reminded me that they don't speak for Jesus. He would look carefully at me, spreading peanut butter onto my sandwich, and tell me he worries about me. Then he'd try to save my soul.

Maldonado usually turns to the church for spiritual guidance. But in the months leading up to the trial, he feared his presence would only lead to confrontation. He sneaked in late to church, sliding into a back pew. He worshipped with the rest of the congregation, listening to the sermon. But when all heads bowed for the closing prayer, Maldonado and his wife slipped quietly back out the door.

Dover is a place that often doesn't welcome those who are different. Over the years, Kitzmiller grew used to this. She is in her late thirties and has round cheeks and hazel eyes and an unlined face. An office manager for a landscape company, she wears her blond hair softly feathered and dresses conservatively in slacks and jeans. There is nothing in her appearance to indicate she might be anything but a pretty suburban mother. But as a divorced woman, she's long had to deal with disapproving looks and judgmental whispers.

When she became the lead plaintiff, the silent glances of reproach changed to more overt acts of hostility. Women she had known for years saw her in the grocery store and turned their backs. She would say hello, and they would walk past her as if she were invisible.

Then the letters started coming.

In the weeks following the filing of the lawsuit, Kitzmiller and the other parents received mail from around the country. Many letters thanked them for standing up for the First Amendment. For the most part, these writers articulated their points clearly, used proper grammar and correct spelling. Other people wrote angry, rambling denunciations of the lawsuit. These letters were, in almost every case, poorly written and contained atrocious spelling.

A man from Sharon, Pennsylvania, wrote: "God created man in his image. God appeared to Moses as fire. True? Definitely! Breathing and fire are the same chemical process. $C + O_2 = CO_2$. Ninth grade science. Food is the fuel we add to our fire. We put the food ashes in a commode. If this isn't using science to prove the existence of God, I don't know what is. We, you, are all walking fireplaces."

The parents read these letters to each other and laughed. In a case that wasn't supposed to be about religion, they found it amusing that so many people accused them of hating God. Many of the letters railed against homosexuality. "God made Adam and Eve. Not Adam and Steve." Other writers warned of the days of tribulation and said the parents would be judged.

At December's school board meeting, Alan Bonsell's father, Donald, had stood at the podium and congratulated his son and the other members for improving science education. Donald Bonsell assured them they had the support of the town. Rob Eshbach, the soft-spoken biology teacher and preacher's son, watched Bonsell

from the back of the room. While those in Bonsell's conservative Christian community no doubt backed the board, Eshbach
thought, it didn't mean everyone supported it.

A month later, Eshbach and Chuck Benton, a fellow Dover
educator, assembled a group of Dover residents in the basement
of a Lutheran church just off Dover's square. The plaintiffs were
invited. Kitzmiller attended, along with Cyndi Sneath, Steve
Stough, and Bryan Rehm.

The two teachers told those in the room that Dover's battle
couldn't just be fought in the courtroom. They said they needed
to take their fight to the election booth. That year, seven of the
nine pro–intelligent design board members, including Alan Bonsell and Sheila Harkins, were up for election.

Eshbach and Benton suggested that the group should orga-
nize a slate of candidates to run against board members. They
came up with a name for their political action committee: Dover
CARES, an acronym for Citizens Actively Reviewing Educational Strategies.

For Eshbach, Dover CARES was a leap of faith—faith in his
community, faith in this country's system of democracy, faith
that the people Eshbach had known all his life felt as he did, that
teaching their children about religion was a right that belonged
only to them.

Benton is a conservative Christian, but he disapproved of the
school board's tactics. He teaches drafting to industrial arts students. Like Eshbach, he graduated from Dover High. Despite
Eshbach's more liberal religious views, he and Benton leaned
on each other for spiritual support. Once a week, in the early
morning before school began, the two men met for Bible study in
Eshbach's classroom. They read scripture related to strength and
leadership. Eshbach keeps one of his favorite verses, 1 Timothy
4:12, scrawled in the front of his date book: "*Let no man despise thy*

youth; but be thou an example of the believers, in word, in conversation, in charity, in spirit, in faith, in purity."

In the weeks after the meeting, residents stepped forward to run for school board. Bernie Reinking, a fifty-eight-year-old nurse and wife of a former Dover administrator, volunteered first. Her four children all graduated from Dover schools, and her family was well known in the community. Others joined her: a school bus driver, a nursing home administrator, and a Vassar-educated English major and her businessman husband. In addition to being a plaintiff, Bryan Rehm asked to be a candidate.

No one in the group had any political experience, but they pooled their strengths. Those who didn't run for office helped in other ways. Plaintiff Cyndi Sneath handled communications and researched election regulations. Another person kept track of events. Yet another drafted press releases. Benton ran the weekly meetings.

The community support that Eshbach put his faith in didn't always exist. While campaigning, Reinking knocked on an older man's door. The man, recognizing her, jumped up and down like a monkey. He hooted like an ape and scratched his sides. "Sir, be careful," Reinking told him, alarmed. "I'm a nurse, you could give yourself a heart attack."

Another man, professing to be a Christian, slammed a door in Bryan Rehm's face. Through the open window, Rehm heard him say, "Asshole."

Mothers pulled their daughters out of Beth Eveland's Girl Scout troop. They didn't want their girls associating with atheists, she was told. Rumors circulated that Dover CARES stood for Citizens Against Religious Education in Schools.

Neighbors turned their backs on each other, pretending not to see each other from across their backyards. Others stopped taking evening walks to avoid the cold stares and unreturned waves.

People learned to keep their heads down at the grocery store. Children of some of the plaintiffs were teased. Plaintiff Julie Smith's daughter came home from school one day and asked her mother how she could say she believed in evolution and still believe in God.

Before he would speak to a reporter, Pastor Ed Rowand had a firm policy.

Appointed to the school board to fill a vacancy after the Browns quit, he became one of the board's most vocal members, speaking out in support of the intelligent design policy.

I called Rowand from the newsroom one evening to talk about the Fox News video in which Buckingham explicitly endorsed creationism. Rowand, however, only wanted to talk about my faith. This was the condition of his interviews. Reporters first had to divulge their religious views. I refused. I said it was none of his business, especially since intelligent design wasn't supposed to be about religion. But with Rowand, everything leads back to God. He refused to talk to me until I changed my mind. If we couldn't talk about religion, Rowand wasn't interested.

Rowand preaches at the Rohler's Assembly of God, a Pentecostal church in the Conewago Hills. The cemetery plot behind the church is filled with family names of people who settled the area—Krones, Lemkeldes, Hoovers. The family of my second-grade teacher is buried there.

Rowand grew up on Long Island and still has a touch of the accent to prove it. His hometown was a busy place with sidewalks and traffic and subdivisions. Despite his suburban roots, he feels part of Dover. He is a large, beefy man in his mid-forties with blue eyes, a thick mustache, and an easy, wide grin. In front of the pulpit, he is relaxed and warm, moving easily from discussions of Elijah and the false prophets to soliciting prayer chains for the elderly. But away from church, Pastor Rowand loses his grace. Because of his large size, he often appears awkward and uncomfortable.

Rowand was righteous about his belief that civil liberty should be subject to a majority-rules mentality. He was confident, certainly, that most Dover citizens embraced the board's intelligent design policy. In his first election race, Rowand had few doubts that the school board incumbents would beat their challengers.

The board members were all Republicans. Dover CARES candidates, however, were neatly split, half Republican, half Democrat. In Pennsylvania school board primaries, state election law permits those running for school board director to cross-file with both parties. Eighteen candidates vied for seven available seats. (A few months later, both sides would have to find another candidate to run in the fall election after Bill Buckingham quit.)

In May's primary, voters whittled the field down to fourteen, choosing seven from each side. The seven incumbents filled the Republican slate. The seven Dover CARES candidates won the Democratic nomination. Dover was divided.

In the weeks leading up to Dover's trial, President George Bush said publicly that he is among those who question evolutionary theory and supports teaching intelligent design. He told reporters, "Both sides ought to be properly taught . . . so people can understand what the debate is about." He added, "Part of education is to expose people to different schools of thought. . . . You're asking me whether or not people ought to be exposed to different ideas, and the answer is yes."[1]

His position contradicted that of his own science adviser, John H. Marburger, who had said a few months earlier that intelligent design is not a scientific concept.

But Bush was reflecting the views of many Americans. Forty-five percent of people in this country believe that "God created human beings pretty much in their present form at one time within the last 10,000 years." Only about one third of the public believes that evolution is well supported by evidence.[2]

The public's views are in striking contrast to those of scientists. While scientists may debate the details of the engine that drives evolution, they don't dispute that all life on earth is the result of evolutionary forces. Veteran science reporters such as the *New York Times*'s Cornelia Dean have no qualms about making the context clear: "Darwinian evolution is the foundation of modern biology. While researchers may debate details of how the mechanism of evolution plays out, there is no credible scientific challenge to the underlying theory."

In a June 21, 2005, article about the fight over evolution in Kansas, Dean addressed intelligent design proponents' seemingly reasonable argument that public schools should "teach the controversy" with the added explanation: "In theory, this position— 'teach the controversy'—is one any scientist should support. But mainstream scientists say alternatives to evolution have repeatedly failed the tests of science, and the criticisms have been answered again and again. For scientists, there is no controversy."

So why isn't the message getting through to the public? One of the problems is that few newspaper reporters possess backgrounds in science. Furthermore, the mainstream media's adherence to a notion of objectivity and "fair and balanced" journalism is frequently exploited, allowing advocacy organizations to portray an issue as controversial when it's not. Journalists, fearing offending conservative and fundamentalist readers, have become timid at presenting information. Consequently, what passes for news gathering becomes what *Science* magazine's Donald Kennedy called the "two-card Rolodex problem."

"There's a very small set of people who question the consensus," Kennedy said. "And there are a great many thoughtful reporters in the media who believe that in order to produce a balanced story, you've got to pick one commentator from side A and one commentator from side B."[3]

As Bill Kovach and Tom Rosenstiel wrote in their book *The Elements of Journalism,*

> Rather than high principles, [fairness and balance] are really techniques—devices—to help guide journalists in the development and verification of their accounts. They should never be pursued for their own sake or invoked as journalism's goal. Their value is in helping to get us closer to more thorough verification and a reliable version of events.
>
> "Balance, for instance, can lead to distortion. If an overwhelming percentage of scientists, as an example, believe that global warming is a scientific fact, or that some medical treatment is clearly the safest, it is a disservice to citizens and truthfulness to create the impression that the scientific debate is equally split. Unfortunately, all too often journalistic balance is misconstrued to have this kind of almost mathematical meaning, as if a good story is one that has an equal number of quotes from two sides. As journalists know, often there are more than two sides to a story. And sometimes balancing them equally is not a true reflection of reality.[4]

Initially the term "objectivity" wasn't supposed to apply to journalists. When the journalist Walter Lippmann coined it in the 1920s, he was calling for an objectivity of method. Lippmann called on the profession to acquire more of "the scientific spirit," saying that objectivity is the "unity of method rather than aim; the unity of disciplined experiment."[5] He was suggesting a way of setting aside our biases to get to the truth. He was saying that objectivity is the reporter's version of the scientific method.

In the September/October 2005 issue of the *Columbia Journalism Review*, Chris Mooney and Matthew C. Nisbet took the media to task for its failure to be more assertive in the public debate over evolution. Referencing the Dover case, they wrote,

> As evolution, driven by such events, shifts out of scientific realms and into political and legal ones, it ceases to be covered by context-oriented science reporters and is instead bounced to political pages, opinion pages, and television news. And all these venues, in their various ways, tend to deemphasize the strong scientific case in favor of evolution and instead lend credence to the notion that a growing 'controversy' exists over evolutionary science. This notion may be politically convenient, but it is false.

The Discovery Institute's Center for Science and Culture touts itself as "the nation's leading think-tank exploring the scientific theory of intelligent design." To my scientifically illiterate brain, the organization sounded impressive at first.

But in the months after my first exposure to intelligent design, I learned much about the science, culture, and history of the battle over evolutionary theory. My initial enthusiasm for proof of God's existence waned and turned to skepticism. Still, as I sifted through the evidence, I continued to present both sides, trying to maintain my journalistic integrity and provide context for other arguments.

I found those supporting evolution to be friendly and willing to help me understand the issues. I spent long hours on the

phone with many different scientists, who patiently indulged my
uninformed questions. However, when I spoke with members of
the Discovery Institute, they treated my questions with hostility.
Most of my conversations were with John West, Discovery's primary media spokesman, and Jonathan Wells, the author of *Icons of
Evolution*. Wells belongs to the Unification Church and once said
he was directed by the Reverend Sun Myung Moon to "destroy
Darwinism."[6]

One of the ways Wells and others with the Discovery Institute
obfuscate is by fueling public misunderstanding of the scientific
consensus. Intelligent design proponents also argue that the intelligent designer doesn't necessarily mean that the designer is God
and that, perhaps, it could be space aliens. They say that empirical
data supports evidence for design, just as we detect human design
when we look at Mount Rushmore.

They stress the fact that evolution is just a theory.

But as Harvard paleontologist and evolutionary biologist Stephen Jay Gould once explained, "Well, evolution is a theory. It is
also a fact. And facts and theories are different things, not rungs
in a hierarchy of increasing certainty. Facts are the world's data.
Theories are structures of ideas that explain and interpret facts."

At its most simple, evolution is a process that results in changes
in a population that take place over many generations. Those
changes can eventually lead to the transition of one species into
another. Man, for instance, evolved from apes. Five to seven million years ago, our ancestral evolutionary tree diverged into two
branches, one branch developing into chimpanzees and bonobos
and the other branch developing into humans. One of the most
common misunderstandings of human evolution is the idea that
we descended from monkeys. While humans and monkeys share
a common ancestor, our relatives parted ways, scientists estimate,
twenty-five to thirty million years ago.

Intelligent design's proponents refer to "Darwinism" or the spookier "neo-Darwinism" when they speak of evolutionary theory. But Darwin didn't develop either the concept of evolution or the concept of common descent. In fact, scientists were debating the issues long before Darwin wrote *The Origin of Species*. His contribution to modern evolutionary theory was that he was the first to develop fully the idea of natural selection as a major mechanism that accounted for evolutionary change. Darwin allowed us to see how evolution was possible.

Darwin developed his ideas based on observing the breeding of different animals, particularly pigeons and dogs. If over generations artificial selection could create such variability within different species, giving us everything from the Great Dane to the Pekinese, couldn't one extrapolate that the selective pressures in nature might produce similar results on all life over millions of years?

Natural selection is essentially the idea that certain traits provide a creature with a competitive advantage over others in its population, making it better suited to surviving in its environment. Having this competitive advantage allows the creature to pass on its genetic material to a greater number of offspring favored with the same selective advantage. Over time, these continuous incremental changes might lead to one species' diverging into another.

Critics of evolution contend that random processes cannot account for the diversity of life. But natural selection, in and of itself, is the opposite of random. Rather, it is spurred by natural forces and environmental pressure. What Darwin referred to as random variation is today what scientists understand to be caused by genetic mutations. Most of the time, a mutation doesn't provide the creature with a selective advantage, but once in a while, the new genetic material will give it an adaptive and nonrandom advantage over the other creatures in its population.

Advantage is the idea that a mutation might enable a cheetah to run faster and catch more prey, allowing it to live longer and make more babies. Those babies that possess that mutation are more likely to be faster than those in other litters and will be able to catch more prey and pass on their genes. At the same time, those cheetahs without the faster-running gene won't be able to compete as effectively and will be less likely to pass on their genetic material.

Often referred to, although not entirely accurately, as "survival of the fittest," it's like the old joke about two hikers who come across a grizzly bear in the wilderness. The one man tells the other he's going to run. "Run?" his friend says. "You'll never be able to run faster than a grizzly bear."

"I don't have to," the man says, as he takes off. "I just have to run faster than you."

If Dover's battle had been over quantum physics or (God forbid!) string theory, I would have been utterly, hopelessly lost. But evolutionary theory and natural selection are fairly intuitive concepts. As the famed geneticist Theodosius Dobzhansky wrote in 1973, "Nothing in biology makes sense except in the light of evolution."

So when Wells argued, as he did in *Icons of Evolution*, that Galapagos finches' beaks make a poor example of evolution, I grasped the fallacy in his argument. While Wells acknowledges that the finches are a great example of natural selection at work, he argues that the small changes witnessed through environmental adaptation don't make a case for macroevolution, the change from one species to another.

In *Icons*, he points to a mid-1990s study in which, during periods of drought, the finches' beaks became bigger from season to season, adapting to the tougher nuts that grew on the island. But he discounts natural selection by saying that when the rains return, the beaks tend to grow smaller again, or more varied, from generation to generation. The result is that there has been no "net" evolution, he says. Rather, the changes are "washed out," he says, because the beak sizes vary depending on the amount of rain over the years. While watching the video, even I realized that Wells completely missed the point. The size of the beaks varies precisely because of adaptations to environmental pressures— natural selection at work. But Wells failed to mention that in a sustained drought, the beak size would likely remain large as the finches adapted to their new environment. Eventually, under the principles of Darwin's theory, the beak size would become fixed in the population and a new species of finch would evolve. In one of our more testy exchanges, Wells said I was wrong and that his assertion is correct. If the drought continued, he said, macro-evolution could still not occur. "All the birds would have died," Wells snapped. "Period. End of story. No evidence."

Bill Buckingham briefly went to Dover High School, where in typing class he met the woman he'd eventually marry. "She had the prettiest blue eyes I've ever seen," he remembers. But he didn't have the nerve to ask her out then. He moved away and transferred to York High. Soon after his graduation, he ran into Charlotte again. Given a second chance, he didn't let her got away. "You can call me," she told him. They've been married for forty years and have three children, six grandchildren, and two great-grandchildren.

I like the Bill Buckingham that he usually shows me, the one who likes to talk about bluegrass music and his beloved Philadelphia Phillies and his hero Richie Ashburn, the one who tells great stories and pats me on the hand and treats me like a daughter. But there is a sadness to him, too. He weaves stories of his father, who lived with him for six years before he died. His father grew up near Baltimore, the forgotten son of a man who had two families.

Buckingham says his father got drunk only once a year, on Christmas Day, because on that day during World War II, in the Philippines, he had watched his fellow Marines get slaughtered by the Japanese. His father was also at Pearl Harbor and on duty the morning of December 7 and stared into the eyes of a Japanese fighter pilot strafing American G.I.s.

A musician, Buckingham says he used to play for his father while Charlotte sang along. But after his father died, he said, he sold his Martin guitar and hasn't played since.

As a cop, Buckingham shot a man twice and he shot a dog once. The man was robbing a house and attacked Buckingham in the dark. Buckingham defended himself, he said. The dog had been badly injured when struck by a car. Buckingham put the animal out of its misery.

In his living room, surrounded by pictures of his grandchildren, crocheted doilies, and his wirehaired Yorkie named Whitey, Buckingham said to me, "I didn't mind shooting the man, but I sure felt bad about shooting the dog."

I'm aware of Buckingham's other side. The side that gets angry, and arrogant. He wears a police officer's buzz cut and has blue eyes the color of cornflowers. As he talks, those eyes meet your gaze—almost defiantly, challenging you not to believe him—before his glance darts away, looking around the room, at the floor, the wall behind you, at Whitey.

In the months leading up to the trial, Richard Thompson began to hint at his defense strategy. He continued to uphold his clients' assertions that they never spoke publicly of creationism and that the newspaper reporters were biased. But at the same time, he said that if creationist remarks had been made, they were made by a man addicted to OxyContin. The rest of the board, he said, should not be held responsible for Buckingham's behavior.

Buckingham says Thompson told his fellow school board members to distance themselves from him. He grew depressed. One Sunday a few months before the trial began, he picked up his fishing pole and gun, walked out the door, and climbed into his car. He had had a fight with his wife that morning over something trivial. But the pressures of his father's death, his addiction, and his back and knee surgeries had worn on him, he says. Instead of going to church that morning, he drove around York County. He intended to go fishing, he says, but he also intended to kill himself. A chance meeting with his second-grade teacher changed his mind. He drove by her house and knocked on her door. He never mentioned that he was thinking of killing himself. But she reassured him nonetheless.

Soon after he returned home that day, he and Charlotte decided that the pressure had gotten to be too much. Buckingham quit the school board only months before the start of September's trial. He sold his house, and they moved to South Carolina. He said his body could no longer stand Pennsylvania's cold winters.

That spring and summer, I ranted to my father about the school board's deception. He listened with a blank expression. He asked, well, which one is the good side? I understood what he was asking: Which side professed to be on the side of God?

"But they lied, Dad," I said.

"I'd have to hear their side of it," he told me.

My father had not always been a fundamentalist Christian. His religious conversion began with his failing storefront radio station in the tiny borough of Shiremanstown. The story of the radio station formed the cornerstone of his testimony, of how he turned his life over to Christ.

One's testimony is an integral part of the evangelical movement. It is the basis of leading others to Christ, of delivering salvation. As it says in John 3:3, *"No one can see the kingdom of God unless he is born again."*

To be effective, it must be a good dramatic story of being entered by the holy spirit. There are rules to delivering testimony. The converted may have been either a sinner, or a languishing Christian too tolerant of other faiths. They must speak of the moment of redemption, of being humbled with the knowledge that Christ died for their sins. They must talk of relinquishing control over their lives and turning it all over to God. The testimony, if it's to be credible, must include elements of uncanny coincidences and immediate blessings.

Dean Lebo gave his testimony at Pentecostal churches throughout Pennsylvania. An advertising salesman around Harrisburg, he and his partner came up with the idea for an oldies radio station while drinking one night in a bar. WWII-720 went on the air in 1987. But from the beginning, sales were poor. God was trying to get his attention, but my father ignored him and continued his reckless ways. The radio station limped along for a few years, but when clients pulled their advertising, the station sank into bankruptcy. My father stopped answering the phone—only creditors were calling—and grew depressed. Checks started bouncing, and there were times when my father had barely enough money to pay his employees. The night before the electricity was to be turned off, my father, alone in the station's tiny upstairs apartment where he lived by himself, sank to his knees and prayed. Defeated, he begged God to lift this heavy burden from his shoulders.

The next day, a man representing a local church came in with an offer. In exchange for leasing the radio station, his church would take over the weekday programming.

Overnight, my father became a fundamentalist Christian,

washed in the blood of Christ's loving redemption. It's a good story. It's also pretty much true.

Dean Lebo, his heart filled with proof of God's grace, tried to share his salvation with his children. For years, I played along. It was a nonspoken agreement. As long as he was careful not too make too many demands, I pretended that I believed Jesus died for my sins.

But when he refused to denounce the lying of Dover board members, I felt he was no longer holding up his end of the bargain. If this was what being a Christian demanded, then I wanted no part of it.

In the 1920s, when the nation's eyes were on a Dayton, Tennessee, courtroom as religious fundamentalists challenged the teaching of evolution, Dover's Conewago Hills were a haven for Klansman and bootleggers. Revenuers knew to be cautious when venturing back there. A farmer, wanted for stealing a calf, hid from the law in a place called Bald Hill. When a young police officer knocked on his door, the thief fired his shotgun from his living room, killing the man with a blast to the face.[7]

I was raised in Newberrytown, on the edge of the Conewagos, near the foot of Bald Hill. I am the first of Dean and Ann Lebo's five children.

My mother taught me to love the smell of puppies' milk breath, and the feel of their bellies taut and round like hard-boiled eggs. She taught me to stretch out, my face pressed into the grass, the laundry snapping above me on the clothesline, to indulge in the drowsy feeling of sunshine on the back of my head.

My father pointed to the sky at night and taught me to dream of infinity. On hot summer evenings, he wrestled with his children, like kittens, in the grass until long after the sun went down.

Then, we lay on our backs in the grass and watched the stars. I'd shine a flashlight into the sky, gazing at the beam of light disappearing into the dark. Millions and millions of years from now that light will reach those stars, my father told me. I'd try to follow the beam with my eyes and ponder this until I grew dizzy.

My mother taught me to search within, to take pleasure in the present. My father taught me to imagine possibility.

Our church was built from the red sandstone of farmers' fields. I attended Sunday school each week and sang in the choir. I sat in the pews with my parents and siblings, staring up at a giant blue and gold painting of Christ praying at Gethsemane. I remember almost nothing of the sermons from my childhood, but I can recall almost every detail of that painting, the way Christ's soft hair fell down his back, his blue eyes and long, straight nose, and his pleading expression as he looked into the sky. I later learned in Bible study that the painting depicted Christ's own despair over the prescient knowledge of the next day's torture and crucifixion. "And being in an agony he prayed more earnestly: and his sweat was as it were great drops of blood falling down to the ground." His prayers that night were not for the salvation of man, but for his own mortal flesh.

Every August at Paddletown Church, when the sweet corn and berries were at their peak, the church ladies made Pennsylvania Dutch chicken corn soup and homemade black raspberry ice cream. Because the weather was too hot for cooking and eating inside the non–air-conditioned church, the women worked behind huge kettles set up in a gravel parking lot across the road from the church. The women bobby-pinned their hair into tight buns and, in the hot summer months, wore shapeless and sleeveless house dresses. Each time the ladies, all fat, ladled out a bowl of soup, I watched fascinated as the turkey waddle under their exposed arms swayed back and forth.

As I got older, our family drifted away from the church. My sister Lynn and I still attended occasionally. My parents handed us a dollar bill to put in the collection plate. Sometimes, when the plate was passed, we only pretended to put the money in. Then, we sneaked out early from the service and walked down to the general store to buy candy with God's money.

Still, in those days, I believed in a literal heaven and hell. I accepted that Adam was shaped from dust, that Eve came from a sleeping man's rib, and that Noah was able to pack two of every kind of animal onto his ark. I believed that Jesus died for my sins so that I might have eternal life.

A couple of years later, Baptists from a local church near our house came up with an idea. They bought a school bus, which they drove around local neighborhoods, searching for children out playing in their yards on Sunday mornings. They stopped along the road, swung open the door, and invited us to climb on board.

They had an excuse for every reluctance. It didn't matter if we were barefoot. Jesus walked barefoot. We need to ask our parents. You only need God's permission. From house to house, they continued, until the bus was filled with stolen children. Then, one of the men stood up and began to preach. He told us about hell, a place of eternal suffering, of weeping children and gnashing of teeth. He described a world of burning flesh and tearing limbs.

One spring, the man told us that there was no such thing as the Easter bunny. Santa Claus doesn't exist either. It's OK, the man told the shocked faces, because you can believe in someone greater. Only Jesus can save you from hell.

Soon we learned to run and hide when we saw the bus coming.

7

A Little Constitutional Violation

So keep fightin' for freedom and justice, beloveds, but don't you forget to have fun doin' it.

—*Molly Ivins*

Most mornings, after a late night of preparing for court, Eric Rothschild climbed out of bed before 5:30, filled with excitement, and laced up his running shoes. He stepped out of a squat, brown-brick Harrisburg apartment building that sits amid lawyers' row on Front Street.

For six weeks, the plaintiffs' legal team called the apartment building home. Rothschild and Steve Harvey slept in one apartment. Vic Walczak and Nick Matzke, the plaintiffs' resident science expert, shared another. The forced intimacy became a running joke: Brokeback Attorneys.

The apartments stand next to the Temple Ohev Sholom. Five years earlier, an arsonist set fire to the synagogue's school building on Yom Kippur, the holiest day of the Jewish year—an ever-present reminder of the price of religious intolerance.

With the sun barely over the horizon, Rothschild crossed the street and ran south along a trail overlooking the riffles and islands of the Susquehanna River's shallow waters. If he ran with his head up, he might have noticed steam billowing from the cooling towers of the Three Mile Island nuclear power plant only a few miles farther south.

But Rothschild charged forward with his head down, consumed most mornings by details of the trial. The leaves changed on the sycamores and oaks towering over him as a glorious Indian summer gave way to late autumn. He barely noticed. Sometimes Rothschild crossed the bridge to City Island, home to the Senators, the capital's minor-league baseball team. As he turned around and headed back to Harrisburg, halfway into his four-mile run, he could see the top of the federal courthouse in front of him. On the first day of the trial, television news trucks camped out on the street before dawn. The spacious dwelling of Pepper Hamilton's Harrisburg office stands one block farther south, overlooking the water. Four blocks north, the elegant dome of the state Capitol, where the lawyers and plaintiffs first huddled together and announced their lawsuit, peaks above the horizon.

On the first day of the trial, Rothschild bounded into the courtroom with his characteristic energy and the nervousness of a cocker spaniel puppy. About the same time, I rushed out of my house twelve miles away in northern York County. An insect on the window of my front door caught my attention. In the woods surrounding my house, American walking sticks of the insect order Phasmatodea cling to branches and sway deceptively like twigs in the breeze.

Stretched out three inches long, this walking stick sat unmoving, even as I opened the door. I leaned in to peer at its long brown body and marveled at its uncanny likeness to an actual stick. I picked it up, letting it wander up my wrist. Before each nimble step, it used its grasping claws to explore. When it rested, it stretched out and neatly folded its claws, enhancing its sticklike appearance. I thought of the small, successive genetic mutations over time that provided its camouflage and obvious defense against hungry birds. I dropped it onto a rhododendron leaf and climbed into my car. Why, I wondered, is natural selection so hard for people to understand?

As parents, school board members, lawyers, reporters, and news junkies filed into Courtroom No. 2 that first morning, a woman stood outside the building in judgment. Holding a Bible, she prayed for the salvation of lost Darwinist-believing souls.

At 9 A.M., Judge Jones breezed into the courtroom on the ninth floor of the federal building with long, athletic strides, his robe billowing around his legs. The scattered conversations halted. All faces turned toward him as he took his seat at the front of the courtroom. What Jones saw pulled him up short. He looked out into the packed pews. For the first time, he had a sense of the momentousness of the trial and his role in it.

Until then, Jones's claim to fame had been that he headed the state Liquor Control Board (LCB), where he banned a can of beer bearing the image of a frog flipping off customers with its middle finger.

Jones, who is fifty years old, was born in a small town at the center of Pennsylvania's anthracite coal region. His family owns golf courses, and Jones boasts solid conservative credentials. He is friends with Tom Ridge, who, as the state's Republican governor, appointed him LCB chairman. President George Bush appointed Jones to the federal bench. Rick Santorum, Pennsylvania's far-right conservative and devoutly religious U.S. senator, endorsed him. Santorum also sat on the Thomas More Law Center's advisory board.

Initially, intelligent design supporters speculated enthusiastically that Jones, because of his conservative pedigree, was on their side. On William Dembski's pro-ID blog *Uncommon Descent*, contributor DaveScot wrote,

Judge John E. Jones on the other hand is a good old boy brought up through the conservative ranks. He was state attorney for D.A.R.E, an Assistant Scout Master . . . extensively involved with local and national Boy Scouts of America, political buddy of Governor Tom Ridge (who in turn is deep in George W. Bush's circle of power), and finally was appointed by GW hisself. Senator Rick Santorum is a Pennsylvanian in the same circles (author of the 'Santorum Language' that encourages schools to teach the controversy) and last but far from least, George W. Bush hisself drove a stake in the ground saying teach the controversy. Unless Judge Jones wants to cut his career off at the knees he isn't going to rule against the wishes of his political allies. Of course the ACLU will appeal. This won't be over until it gets to the Supreme Court. But now we own that too.

In court that morning, Jones gave no outward appearance of nervousness, except for a brief pause before speaking: "Good morning to all. Counsel, would you enter your appearances starting with counsel for the plaintiffs."

One by one, the attorneys introduced themselves. Jones looked out over their heads, picking out faces of prominent national journalists. He remembered later that his stomach was filled with butterflies, but he knew he had to pull himself together. "And good morning to all of you," he said.

Parents and scientists sat behind their legal team on Jones's left. The school board members, backed by pastors and other supporters, sat behind their lawyers on his right. Reporters wore designated numbered tags. Because this was a bench trial, there was no jury. Those reporters who came early were rewarded with front-row seats in the jury box. I wore tag No. 1.

Before the trial, I thought I had done my homework. I grasped the idea that intelligent design relies on supernatural explanations, while the study of science, under the guidance of methodological naturalism, limits observations and hypotheses to the natural world. I knew that when intelligent design's supporters say they don't know who the designer is, they do so with a nod and a wink. I knew that there are no peer-reviewed articles in support of intelligent design. I knew that the assertion of "purposeful arrangement of parts" was a rehash of the Reverend William Paley's argument on behalf of a creator, which basically says, If it looks designed, it is designed. I knew that evolutionary theory is the cornerstone of modern biology; that *Pandas and People* was filled with gross inaccuracies about the fossil record, homology, the tree of life, and the principles of common descent. I knew that the human brain can accommodate both scientific knowledge and belief in God.

I understood these concepts. What I hadn't grasped was the depth of the deception defendants were trying to foist on the public. In his opening arguments, Rothschild summed up what I would soon realize: "They did everything you would do if you wanted to incorporate a religious topic in science class and cared nothing about its scientific validity."

Then, Rothschild pointed to the defense's assertion that the curriculum change was so tiny, any constitutional violations could be ignored. "Of course," he pointed out, "there is no such thing as a little constitutional violation."

Patrick Gillen, the school district's attorney and the one who would do the heavy lifting for the defense through most of the trial, followed Rothschild in opening arguments. A slender man with a wide grin, he spoke in a hoarse voice that grew harder to hear as the trial continued. Gillen made the essential points: The revised curriculum was merely "a modest change." Gillen argued that the policy wasn't teaching intelligent design. It was merely making them aware of alternative theories. And he reminded us that evolution is a theory, not a fact.

"The evidence will show that the consistent goal of the board, as a whole, was to pursue what they believed to be a legitimate educational purpose and to comply with the law," Gillen told the court. "Alan Bonsell is a perfect example. He came to the board without any background in education or the law, just a sincere desire to serve his fellow citizens."

Yet, even as he praised Bonsell, Gillen distanced the defense from Buckingham. One of his primary points was that Buckingham did not represent the views of the entire school board. While Gillen mentioned neither Buckingham's OxyContin addiction nor his obvious public statements about creationism, his point was clear. He was setting the stage for what would become two of the defense's recurrent and contradictory themes: No one ever publicly said the word creationism. But, if someone did, they also argued, it was Buckingham, and board members could hardly be blamed for the drug-addled rants of a crazed religious nut.

Dr. Ken Miller was the first witness to testify. Parents' attorneys chose the Brown University biology professor as their lead-off science expert for many reasons, not the least of which were his amiable enthusiasm and polished presentation. He served as the trial's showman.

Because complex concepts are not easily reduced to glib sound bites, scientists often come off as clunky and inarticulate in debates against the sweeping assertions of creationists and intelligent design proponents. Miller is one of a rare breed of scientists who not only are willing to debate the issues but also relish it.

In 1981, in his first year teaching at Brown, his students approached him with a request. Henry Morris, of San Diego's Institute for Creation Research, was giving a talk at the college.

No other professors would debate Morris about his assertions that evolution was a lie. Would Miller get on stage with him? At first he refused, saying he didn't have the background. But the students persisted. "So, does that mean evolution is a lie?" they asked. Miller finally agreed, under the condition that his students had to provide him with everything they could find regarding creationist arguments. Miller anticipated Morris's points and planned his response. If the universe is only six thousand years old, light from distant stars wouldn't have had time to reach us. If Morris is correct about young earth creationism, Miller said, then God would have had to create the light beams in midstream. Why would God try to trick us like that?

Miller also co-wrote one of the most popular biology textbooks in the country: *Biology.* Students know its various versions by the pictures on its cover, such as the "Elephant book" and the "Lion book." Kids in Dover read from the "Dragonfly" edition. Miller is also an expert on "the coupling factor on the thylakoid membrane." He also umpires women's softball.

Thin and tan, Miller hardly fits the image of a geeky laboratory scientist. An athletic-looking man who owns a farm and breeds horses, he has a neatly trimmed beard and striking blue eyes with deep smile lines that crinkle when he's enjoying himself.

In addition to all these attributes, it was no coincidence that the plaintiffs' lead expert held deep religious convictions—a counter to the argument that evolutionary theory is atheistic by nature.

Walczak questioned Miller for the plaintiffs. Walczak has the demeanor of a warhorse who's been through many battles but still enjoys the fight. In his mid-forties, he is slightly bowlegged and sometimes walks stiffly, the result of years spent tearing up his knees on the soccer field.

When he asks a question, Walczak uses his large blue eyes to convey a sense of innocence, both in and out of the courtroom. But there is just the touch of a smirk behind his wide-eyed routine.

Throughout questioning, Walczak reminded Miller to simply explain heady scientific concepts as if he were explaining them to his own mother. But Miller, adept at making the complicated sound simple, hardly needed reminding. "Dr. Miller, isn't evolution just a theory?" Walczak asked at one point in the testimony, emphasizing the word, "just."

Miller answered with the same patience and earnestness he might direct toward a bright but confused student. "Evolution is just a theory," Miller said, "in the same way that the atomic theory of matter is just a theory, the Copernican theory of the solar system is just a theory, or the germ theory of disease is just a theory. But theories . . . are not hunches, they're not unproven speculation. Theories are systems of explanations which are strongly supported by factual observations and which [explain] . . . whole sets of facts and experimental results."

It was like one of those critical expository scenes in a movie. Ostensibly, Miller and Walczak were two actors having a conversation, but one in which crucial plot points were being laid out for the audience. I had a sense that if I went for popcorn during Miller's testimony, I would be lost for the rest of the trial. I scribbled notes furiously.

Only minutes into Miller's testimony, Walczak turned to the courtroom's technical specialist and said, "Could we have the bacterial flagellum PowerPoint?"

Each day, Mike Argento, the *York Daily Record*'s columnist, sat quietly watching from the last seat in the back row of the jury box, filing daily dispatches in the evening. Argento, who has thick white hair and wore jeans every day to court, blended anonymously into the background. But his columns quickly became a hit with the plaintiffs, their lawyers, and scientists. By the end of the trial, they had claimed him as "our Mencken."

In one of his first columns, Argento dubbed the courtroom battle the "Dover Panda Trial," a reference to the *Pandas* textbook. Argento was also paying homage to Mencken, who coined the phrase "Monkey Trial" in the *Scopes* case.

But perhaps the trial should have been nicknamed the "Bacterial Flagellum Trial."

A whiplike appendage that propels a bacteria cell like a tiny outboard motor, the flagellum became part of a recurring debate over one of intelligent design's primary arguments.

So much time was spent discussing the flagellum, Rothschild joked that it became the mascot for the intelligent design movement and that everyone in the trial was required to have at least two pet flagella. At a Halloween party that fall, Christy Rehm, the Bible school–teaching plaintiff, came dressed as one, wearing a little tail poking out of her pants.

The intelligent design movement's brightest star, Dr. Michael Behe, asserts that the bacterial flagellum's working parts are "irreducibly complex" and so could not have arrived through evolutionary processes.

The defense would offer other disputed examples of irreducible complexity—including the blood-clotting cascade of the puffer fish and the human immune system. But to me, the pesky flagellum was the most easily grasped—illustrating perfectly the essential flaw in intelligent design.

The flagellum is a complex system of thirty to forty interworking protein parts. Behe, a biochemist and Lehigh University biology professor, argues that if even one of those working parts is removed, the flagellum's entire system collapses and ceases to function as an outboard motor. This means, he argues, all the working parts must have been snapped together at the same time like a preassembled house of Legos.

As Behe wrote in his book *Darwin's Black Box*, "it would have to arise as an integrated unit, in one fell swoop," rather than by evolution's successive and gradual changes. Behe says this proves that evolutionary processes couldn't be responsible for the system. Therefore, he argues, a designer must have provided the guiding hand.

Behe wouldn't testify for another three weeks, until the defense began presenting its case. But by then, the other side had cast serious doubts about his argument.

In his testimony, Miller explained that one of the problems with Behe's supposition is that just because scientists don't have an answer today, it doesn't mean they won't tomorrow. Miller said Behe's argument boils down to: "Don't bother trying."

There is another problem with the assertion of irreducible complexity, according to Miller. "Dr. Behe rightly points out," he said, "that to imagine such complex systems arising spontaneously in one fell swoop is something that no serious biologist would argue could happen, and I will not argue either. So his point is, as long as irreducible complexity holds, then any system we can identify as irreducibly complex couldn't have been produced by evolution. It's a very, very coherent argument."

But then Miller cheerfully elucidated why it's also not a very good one. In careful detail, Miller outlined a scenario of how an organism's adaptive trait might evolve into another. With ten fewer working protein parts, a flagellum turns into a Type III Protein Secretion System, sort of a tiny hypodermic needle used by certain kinds of bacteria to inject poisons into other cells. This different function, Miller told the court, is an explanation for how a complex system might have evolved through genetic mutation and natural selection. What may have started out as a hypodermic needle may have, over time, evolved through successive and gradual changes into a tiny outboard motor.

The morning of his testimony, Miller had walked into the courtroom wearing a dismantled mousetrap as a tie clip, a visual rebuttal to Behe's argument. Behe frequently uses the mousetrap to demonstrate irreducible complexity—remove any one of the working parts, and the mousetrap ceases to function. Sure, Miller pointed out, it doesn't work as a mousetrap. But remove the locking bar, and it makes a nifty tie clip.

Rothschild eyed the prop warily. Unsure how Judge Jones would react, he told Miller to take it off.

Miller, a Roman Catholic, also spoke passionately about how he is able to reconcile his knowledge of evolution and faith in God. Rather than challenging his religious beliefs, evolution connects him. "The notion that we are united in a great chain of being with every other living thing on this planet confirms my faith in a divine purpose and in a divine plan and means that when I go to church on Sunday, I thank the creator for this wonderful and bounteous Earth and for the process of evolution that gave rise to such beauty and gave rise to such diversity that surrounds us," he said.

He confessed his awful fear that intelligent design could force students to choose between faith and science, that they would abandon curiosity because it makes them question their religion. Or, opting for science, they might turn their back on God.

"Does science consider issues of meaning and purpose in the universe?" Walczak asked.

"To be perfectly honest, no," Miller said. "Scientists think all the time about the meaning of their work, about the purpose of life, about the purpose of their own lives. I certainly do. But these questions, as important as they are, are not scientific questions."

"If I could solve the question of the meaning of my life by doing an experiment in the laboratory, I assure you, I would rush off and do it right now. But these questions simply lie outside the purview of science. It doesn't say they're not important, it doesn't say that any answer to these is necessarily wrong, but it does say that science cannot address it. It's a reflection of the limitation of science."

During a break in Miller's testimony, Pastor Jim Grove hovered outside the courtroom. An ardent creationist, he is a small, wiry man with pale blue eyes and a deeply lined face. He wears tight jeans and cowboy boots and is a recognizable fixture at most local controversial public events. He leads a church outside of Dover and attended the trial most days, sitting on the side of the school board. Every Halloween, he and his parishioners march in the local parade, hoisting grisly photos of aborted fetuses.

One of Grove's targets is the Fairie Fest, an event held in York County each year, a place for pagans and free spirits to dress up as sparkly, winged fairies and dance to the rhythm of drum circles. Last year, Pastor Grove stood outside the festival with signs informing the children passing by that the fairies were going to hell. Larry J. Sanders, a devoutly earnest hippie type with long brown hair, saw what Pastor Grove and his church congregants were doing. He put on his white Jesus robe and stood next to Grove. He told the children that Pastor Grove was wrong. He told them that Jesus loves the fairies. And he told them that Jesus would like to apologize to all the pagans killed over the years in his name.

I've known Pastor Grove for years, and despite his narrow-mindedness, I grudgingly still find something likable about him. He certainly bears the courage of his convictions. Pastor Grove would never lie in the name of Jesus. A Mennonite farmer I know tells me that he believes Pastor Grove will make it to heaven. But it will be such an exclusive place that he will spend eternity alone. In Pastor Grove's small world, everyone is going to hell.

During breaks in the trial, Grove made himself politely available to the media. Seeking local color, every new reporter at the trial approached him for an easy interview. But after only a few minutes, the journalists' faces went slack with boredom. With Pastor Grove, it was always the same speech. He caught me at the water fountain to talk about Miller's testimony. "I don't understand how that man can call himself a Christian," Grove said.

He explained that you can't be a Christian if you believe anything other than the literal word of the Bible. But, I asked, if Miller says he's been able to reconcile that, shouldn't you, as a Christian, be able to take him at his word?

No, Pastor Grove told me, of course not.

Casey Luskin, a staff attorney with the Discovery Institute, lingered near reporters, offering them press releases with a timid smile. Luskin is in his early twenties and has large dark eyes. He didn't have much to say, other than that everything said in the courtroom was wrong.

He argued that the plaintiffs' legal team was spinning the lie that intelligent design was repackaged creationism. He reminded reporters that they should be using what he called Discovery's definition of intelligent design: The theory of intelligent design holds that certain features of the universe and living things are best explained by an intelligent cause, not an undirected process such as natural selection. Intelligent design theory does not claim that science can determine the identity of the intelligent cause.

He argued that intelligent design offers positive evidence. When asked to provide the proof, he recited intelligent design's definition. He said we infer design in biology just as we do with man-made systems.

"All intelligent design can do as a scientific theory is try to identify whether certain features of the natural world are the products of intelligence," Luskin repeated.

He spent a few days at the trial. Then he disappeared.

While Miller testified, two reporters wrestled with a difficult decision a block away in a conference room in the Hilton Hotel. Heidi Bernhard-Bubb and Joe Maldonado, the two freelance correspondents accused of lying in their news accounts of the June 2004 board meetings, were trying to decide whether to testify or face contempt of court charges.

In the weeks before the trial, the decision weighed heavily on them. With the *New York Times* reporter Judith Miller sitting in a jail cell for refusing to divulge her source in the Valerie Plame case, they knew what might happen if they refused to take the stand. Maldonado woke up each morning before dawn, unable to sleep. He thought of his finances, of how he'd have to close his sandwich shop if he went to prison. Bernhard-Bubb, still nursing her infant daughter, fretted over who would care for her children. She had long talks with her husband. If she went to jail, he might have to take off work.

Unlike Judith Miller, Maldonado and Bernhard-Bubb were not well-paid staff reporters. They would collect no salaries in jail. They covered tiny school districts such as Dover, and were hardworking correspondents who hadn't pondered what it would be like to be thrust into the spotlight of a national story. Still, even though they didn't work for a big international newspaper, they were journalists—journalists who took their responsibilities seriously. They feared their testimony could compromise their role as neutral observers. They feared the impact this might have for journalists in similar cases.

It became a sticky First Amendment side issue to the trial's First Amendment battle.

Bernhard-Bubb, in her late twenties, was then the mother of two children, a three-year-old son and seven-month-old daughter. She still had the feminine curves of a woman who gave birth not too long ago. She has luminescent skin and light blonde hair. She was born in Kalamazoo, Michigan, and pursued an English degree at Brigham Young University. She remains one semester shy of her degree and hopes to return to school one day, perhaps when her children are older. She and her husband are Mormons.

Maldonado, in his late thirties, grew up in a working-class section of York, just south of Dover. He was raised a Baptist and started the Bible club at York High. He spent a semester at Jerry Falwell's Liberty University before leaving to join the Air Force.

The remarks about creationism were central to the plaintiffs' assertion that the intelligent design statement violated the First Amendment's Establishment Clause. The words made clear that board members' motivation was to get creationism into science class. Under the requirements spelled out by the U.S. Supreme Court in the 1971 case of *Lemon v. Kurtzman*, legislation must meet three criteria to pass constitutional muster: 1) the government's action must have a legitimate secular purpose; 2) the government's action must not have the primary effect of either advancing or inhibiting religion; 3) the government's action must not result in an "excessive goverment entanglement" with religion. These criteria are known as the "Lemon test," and if legislation does not meet all three, it is a violation of the Establishment Clause and is unconstitutional. Plaintiffs' attorneys said they would be happy with the newspaper's request to have the reporters sign affidavits swearing to the accuracy of their articles. But the defense wanted to be able to question the reporters, to ask them about their biases.

Walczak, meanwhile, agonized over what he and his colleagues were doing. As an ACLU attorney, he has fought, many times, for the rights of journalists. But in this case, he was fighting to force them to testify. Walczak declined colleagues' offers to be the public face for him, knowing he couldn't avoid the inevitable criticism. It was his battle.

Because of board members' denials, attorneys feared that even with numerous witnesses testifying that they heard the creationist remarks, Judge Jones might still question their religious motivations. Walczak believed they needed the sworn statements of reporters.

In his first order, Judge Jones said Maldonado and Bernhard-Bubb could be questioned about their biases and prejudices. Then, in an effort at compromise, Jones changed the order to limit questioning to only what they saw and heard. That still left the reporters vulnerable to interrogating questions outside the realm of their reporting and could compromise their neutrality.

The morning of his scheduled deposition, Maldonado awoke with the word "contempt" pounding in his head. He dressed in his black suit and drove to the hotel for the deposition. Maldonado sat down at a table with Ed White, one of Dover's attorneys, who promptly started asking questions. Each time, in response, Maldonado said, "I'm going to invoke my rights under reporter's privilege."

After only about five minutes, White gave up. "Are you aware you could be held in contempt?" he asked. Maldonado said he understood that this was true.

Next it was Bernhard-Bubb's turn. As she headed into the conference room, she told the waiting reporters she was still mulling over her decision. Ten minutes later, she emerged. Like Maldonado, she had refused to answer White's questions.

That night, Maldonado and Bernhard-Bubb went to bed not knowing what would happen to them in the morning. The next day, attorney Niles Benn, representing both newspapers, met privately with Jones, urging him to reconsider. After forty-five minutes, Jones finally agreed to change his order. The reporters still had to testify, but only to "what was seen and heard (at the board meetings) as related in the newspaper articles." No one would go to jail.

Dr. Robert Pennock, the expert witness to follow Miller, told the court that intelligent design proponents have deeper motives than just getting their concept into biology class. They want nothing less than to return science to the days of pre-Enlightenment.

Pennock, a philosophy of science professor at Michigan State University, outlined what he argues is the movement's ultimate goal: to create a revolution in science, taking it back to the days when people believed epilepsy was caused by divine possession and gravity was the result of "spooky action at a distance."

Genial and enthusiastic, Pennock loves talking about concepts that most people can barely comprehend. In his cross-examination by Gillen, Pennock explained that in some ways creation science is more scientific than intelligent design. Even though its tenets have all been refuted by the scientific community, creation science at least puts forth arguments that are testable, such as the idea that the earth is six thousand years old and that the geological record was formed by the Great Flood.

But intelligent design departs from testable claims, such as assertions of the earth's age, and relies solely on supernatural explanations. In this way, it can't be falsified, he told the court.

Then Pennock, leaning forward in his chair, said, "For all we know, the world may have been created five minutes ago and we've just been implanted with memories to make us think that it's much longer, right?"

Argento, in his column the next day, wrote, "And thus did intelligent design somehow join the wow-have-you-ever-looked-at-your-hand-I-mean-really-looked school of stoner intellectual epistemology."

Only three days into the trial, and any thoughts I had that this would be a dry recitation of boring scientific facts dissipated. This was . . . fun. Journalists, parents, spectators—even Judge Jones—leaned forward during testimony, fascinated by the science and civic lessons.

When trying to understand heady concepts, we'd press our hands to our eyes and shake our heads. During breaks, so as not to miss a minute of testimony but wanting to stay alert, reporters ran for coffee at a shop two blocks away and gulped it down, still hot, moments before the sheriff's deputies closed the doors and the trial resumed.

From my perch in the jury box, I looked into the courtroom pews to gauge the responses to a piece of testimony I didn't understand. I was struck by the fact that not everyone in the courtroom was engaged. School board members and their supporters were disinterested. Sheila Harkins and Heather Geesey were blank; their faces rarely changed expression. Pastor Rowand sat slump-shouldered, his eyes heavy-lidded, about to fall asleep. Often his mouth hung open. Only Bonsell wore a steady, serene smile—no matter how damaging the testimony. I wondered, "What is he thinking about?"

In between the expert testimony, teachers spoke of board members looking over their shoulders, of bullying them to teach creationism. Parents took the stand, telling poignant stories of their own children questioning their belief in God because they believed in evolution, of being shunned by neighbors and of being told they were going to hell. The teachers and parents also spoke of sitting through June 2004 board meetings, of listening to board members talk about creationism and Christianity.

"I remember comments about our country being founded on Christianity and not needing to teach the faiths of other people," Christy Rehm testified. "And I remember talking to my husband

about that in the car ride home as well, because we're both teachers and I was—when I hear things like that, I immediately think
of my students, and I was thinking about the diverse group of students that I have in my classroom, who all have different religious
viewpoints, and how difficult that would be to tell one student
that, you know, we can't express your belief, but we can express
that person's belief in the classroom. And I just find those things
to be very upsetting when I hear things like that being said."

Barrie Callahan, whose question regarding the purchase of new
biology books prompted the religious discussion at the meetings,
remembered it clearly. "Bill Buckingham talked about creationism," she said. "Alan Bonsell talked about creationism."

Because Thompson rebuffed plaintiffs' attorneys' request to accept that all eleven parents had legitimate standing, every one of
them had to testify. Plaintiffs' attorneys had intended to put only
Kitzmiller on the stand. But Thompson wanted the right to cross-
examine them all, to ask them how they had been harmed by the
intelligent design policy.

His insistence that they all testify led to some of the trial's most
powerful remarks, for neither Cyndi Sneath nor Fred Callahan,
the reticent paper company executive, would otherwise have been
thrust on the stand.

Callahan, now in his late fifties, grew up in York County and
met his wife in college. He brought her home to Dover, where
they've lived since, in a hilltop home overlooking the valley.
He wears well-tailored Navy blazers and combs his dark hair
neatly in a side part. In a crowd of Rotarians, he would blend in
perfectly.

Speaking softly, Callahan's testimony had been unremarkable
until Harvey asked, "Can you tell us how you've been harmed?"

Callahan began to list the ways his rights had been infringed upon: He's a taxpayer and this is a waste of money; he and his wife had been called atheists even though they aren't.

He paused. Angry, he nonetheless continued in an even and measured voice. "We're said to be intolerant of other views," he said, moving his hands. "Well, what am I supposed to tolerate? A small encroachment on my First Amendment rights? Well, I'm not going to. I think this is clear what these people have done. And it outrages me."

Barrie Callahan had promised their daughter that she would go to her field hockey game and was not in the courtroom that day. But others who were there have told her, many times, of the way his words gave them chills, this measured assertion of strength and patriotism.

It was a Frank Capra moment. Rothschild, watching from the attorneys' table, took notice. The seemingly impromptu speech reminded him of what was at stake. Callahan's words brought home that the First Amendment was not just some legal document to be dissected and debated by lawyers. It belonged to quiet men and women, regular citizens who hold dear their right to express their views.

Cyndi Sneath followed Callahan.

Sneath has round blue eyes and fair skin. She looks a little like Cindy Lou Who with a Joan Jett haircut. She is the one, as she likes to say, who cuts through the bullshit. But there is a vulnerability to her that she tries to hide behind her tough-girl demeanor.

She had always hated speaking in public. A tough, independent-minded woman, she nonetheless insisted on remaining in the background during the trial. She hid from reporters by smoking cigarettes outside the courthouse's back door. In high school, when assigned oral presentations, she skipped the day they were due, preferring a failing grade to getting up in front of the class.

When Sneath came into court the day she was to testify, she was shaking. She considered wearing a nicotine patch to help calm her nerves. Instead, she smoked walking from Pepper Hamilton's office to the courthouse.

"I'm probably going to be your worst witness," she told Walczak as the two rode the elevator up to the courtroom. He reassured her. "It's just a conversation," he said. "Just look at me. We'll just be having a conversation."

As she was about to take the stand, Gillen turned to her, gave her a big toothy smile, and told her she would be fine. Sneath was stunned by the support from the defendants' side. It made her think, "Maybe I will be OK."

During her testimony, Sneath did not take her eyes from Walczak's face. After five minutes, her nervousness left her. She felt composed.

She described her son Griffin's love of science, of how when she needs a break, she puts on a television show about NASA. Griffin will be glued to the TV until it's over. Then, just as all the other parents had been asked, Walczak asked Sneath, "Do you believe you've been harmed by what the Dover Area School District has done in promoting intelligent design?"

"Yeah," Sneath said, nodding her head. "I do."

"And how have you been harmed?" he asked.

"Well, you know, as a parent, you want to be proactive in your child's education. I mean, obviously I'm not an educator. I have no big degrees. I want to be proactive, but I depend on the school district to provide the fundamentals. And I consider evolution to be a fundamental of science. And I'm quite concerned about a cautionary statement. I am quite concerned about this intelligent design idea. I do think it's confusing. I don't think it adds to his education.

"And at the end of the day, I mean, in my mind, intelligent designer, I mean, the word 'designer' is a synonym for Creator, and, you know, that takes a leap of faith for me, you know."

Sneath tipped her head to the side and smiled. "And I think it's my privilege to guide them in matters of faith, not a science teacher, not an administrator, and not the Dover Area School Board."

My eyes went from Sneath to her attorneys. Walczak stood staring at her for a moment, a slightly stunned smile on his face. Rothschild and Harvey, sitting at the attorneys' table, both rested their chins in their hands, silly grins on their faces, as they gazed up at Sneath.

Each morning, on my drive to Harrisburg, I called my father on my cell phone. I'd tell him about what happened in court the day before and what was likely to happen that morning. He never seemed to care. But that didn't keep me from pointing out, in each conversation, about the lying on behalf of Jesus. "They showed the tape of Bill Buckingham saying they should be teaching creationism in science class, Dad."

"Well, shouldn't they be teaching it?" he'd say. I'd demand to know where it says in the Bible that lying is OK. He'd just laugh at me. Or ask me about school prayer. Or Bill Clinton. It always got back to Bill Clinton. I'd become furious and hang up. The next morning, I'd call him again.

One morning, already late for trial, the argument continued as I parked my car in the garage across from the courthouse. Like many reporters I know, I have a car filled with newspapers, notebooks, dirty clothing, and Styrofoam coffee cups. As I scrambled to find a pen, my cell phone still pressed to my ear, I dropped my car keys amid the trash and paper. "Shit," I told my father. "I gotta go. I can't find my keys."

Rather than letting me get off the phone, as I frantically threw things over my head and into the back seat, searching for the lost keys, he asked me to sit still for a minute. "I want to pray for them," he said. I sighed and told him to make it quick.

A few moments later, the keys appeared. For me, it hardly qualified as a miracle. But for my father, it was undeniable proof of God's intervention. I paused. "Thanks, Dad." I knew what he'd say next. "Thank God," he told me.

"Thank you, God."

That morning, as I said goodbye, I told my father I loved him. He said he loved me. Then I sprinted for the courthouse. Out of breath, I slipped through the door, just as the sheriff's deputies were closing it. I rushed to my seat, glancing to my right at the plaintiffs. I wondered how many of them had been prayed over that morning. I thought, "Well, if this turns out all wrong, at least there's someone lobbying on my behalf."

8

Where Every House Is a Palace

Creation means that the various forms of life began abruptly through the agency of an intelligent creator with their distinctive features already intact—fish with fins and scales, birds with feathers, beaks, and wings, etc.

—*Of Pandas and People,* 1986 edition

Each morning, Walczak and Nick Matzke climbed into the lawyer's car for the two-mile drive to the courthouse. A Bruce Springsteen collection rotated continuously in the CD player. Before pulling out into traffic, Walczak ritually punched the button for track 14, filling the car with the words: *"They prosecuted some poor sucker in these United States. For teaching that man descended from the apes."*

For Walczak, a New Jersey boy, Springsteen had become something of the trial's patron saint.

A few weeks before the trial began, as reported in *Esquire* magazine, Springsteen introduced his song, "Part Man, Part Monkey," at a concert in Newark by saying "Dover, PA—they're not sure about evolution. Here in New Jersey, we're countin' on it."

For the plaintiffs' team, this was exciting news. But for Walczak, who still dreams of meeting Springsteen, and Kevin Padian, a paleontologist also raised in New Jersey, this was incredible. Dover made it onto the Boss's radar.

But then Padian, who would testify about the fossil record, felt like he had been preparing for this case his whole professional life.

An evolutionary biologist, his dissertation described the evolution of flight and locomotion in pterosaurs, flying reptiles that lived during the age of dinosaurs. He is a professor at the University of California, Berkeley's, Department of Integrative Biology and curator at its Museum of Paleontology. His research explores how major adaptations—such as the origin of flight or the dinosaurs' domination of the earth—start with evolution. He also researches the history of evolutionary theory. He's written a hundred peer-reviewed papers. But what most impressed Mike Argento was that Padian co-edited and helped write the *Encyclopedia of Dinosaurs*. "How cool is that?" Argento said.

Walczak shared Argento's enthusiasm for dinosaurs and talked excitedly about the day's testimony, despite the fact that he had no science background and majored in philosophy. His wife, Kathy, and three children sat in the courtroom.

In his twenty-five years in California, Padian had exchanged his Jersey accent for a softer Berkeley inflection. He is lanky with a shock of white hair that waves around when he talks.

A die-hard Oakland A's fan, Padian entered the courthouse feeling like pitcher Dennis Eckersley closing the game in the ninth inning. But he maintained a cool yet concerned demeanor. "Evolution of life is essentially the whole enchilada," he testified, explaining how the fossil record connects us to our past.

Under Walczak's questioning, Padian used the facts of the fossil record to weave lovely tales of his adored critters, of the evolution of the whale, of the feathered archaeopteryx.

Scientists believe the whale's ancestor and the ancestor of its first cousin, the hippopotamus, walked the earth for forty million years, munching on plants before dying out in the ice ages, but not before its evolutionary tree diverged—the whale forging into the oceans, the hippopotamus into the African swamps.

The *Pandas* textbook argues that whales' ancestry remains unknown because of huge, unexplainable gaps in the fossil record. But in his testimony, Padian traced the lineage of the whale to its early ancestors, a group of cloven-hoofed mammals, and pointed to numerous transitional fossils illustrating the gradual changes of features along the way as they adapted to the water. Their feet, for instance, grew to be more like flippers. Their limbs grew smaller and eventually separated from their backbones. Their backbones also changed, gradually, into tails used to propel them through the water.

Still, they did not shed their evolutionary history. For in their bodies today, whales possess the remnants of an ankle bone, identical to those found in their hoofed relatives.

Padian also testified about the tremendous amount of evidence that shows that birds evolved from small carnivorous dinosaurs sometime in the late Jurassic period, about 150 million years ago.

Pointing affectionately to an exhibit of a dinosaur called Oviraptor, Padian said, "These white objects you see in this specimen are eggs. And here is the hind limb and the foot on the left side. Here is the hind limb and foot of the right side. Here is part of the tail. And the animal's rib cage is in here. There are more eggs underneath this animal. This critter was brooding its eggs in exactly the same position that hens brood their eggs today."

Padian maintained an air of amiable concern, a conscious approach he and Walczak had rehearsed a week earlier. Padian tried to hold back the contempt he holds for intelligent design, a concept he calls a "malevolent decoy." Padian has said he considers it a ruse to foster confusion and deliberately mislead children, "so that the scales may not fall from their eyes," a reference to Acts 9:18 (*"And immediately there fell from his eyes as it had been scales: and he received sight forthwith, and arose, and was baptized"*).

In his testimony, he summed up his objections by saying, "I think it makes people stupid. I think essentially it makes them ignorant. It confuses them unnecessarily about things that are well understood in science, about which there is no controversy, about ideas that have existed since the 1700s, about a broad body of scientific knowledge that's been developed over centuries by people with religious backgrounds and all walks of life, from all countries and faiths, on which everyone can understand.

"I can do paleontology with people in Morocco, in Zimbabwe, in South Africa, in China, in India—any place around the world. I have co-authors in many countries around the world. We don't all share the same religious faith. We don't share the same philosophical outlook, but one thing is clear, and that is, when we sit down at the table and do science, we put the rest of the stuff behind."

When Walczak asked about the four-paragraph statement read to students, Padian drew on his thirty years of teaching experience, from middle school to graduate school. He compared the division in Dover's community to what would mostly certainly take place in the classroom.

"My sense is that it's very difficult to constrain inquiry just by saying you're going to cut it off, and it's very difficult to say that if you just read a statement it's not going to harm anybody," Padian said. "It's quite clear from the evidence that's been given and from the fact that we're sitting here and by the situation that's developed in Dover, clear from news reports of people arguing with each other, parents arguing with other parents and teachers, teachers arguing with the school board, school board members arguing with each other and quitting, who knows how many bitter conversations have taken place in supermarket aisles and across telephone wires."

★   ★   ★

Richard Thompson is a solidly built man with strong features and dark eyes that flash with intensity. Despite Thompson's previous pronouncements that the case was a "Revolution in Evolution," he didn't seem particularly interested in what was playing out in the courtroom. He spent much of the trial seeming distracted, lost in thought. As Gillen and Muise handled most cross-examinations, he leaned back in his chair, staring at the ceiling and chewing on his tie. He skipped conferences in Jones's chambers, prompting the judge at one point to ask Thompson's co-counsel, "Doesn't he like coming back here?"

Thompson seemed more concerned with how he was perceived by the media than by the judge. When he questioned witnesses, he turned his back on Jones, directing his remarks instead to the jury box filled with reporters. Jones later noted that Thompson's performance for the media was "bad form." One doesn't turn one's back on the judge, especially in a bench trial.

During his questioning of plaintiff Julie Smith, Thompson lectured the woman on her decision to join the lawsuit. "Now, there's a bit of street wisdom, and I don't know whether you agree with this or not, and that street wisdom is, don't believe everything you read in the newspapers," Thompson said. "Have you ever heard that?"

"Yeah, I've heard that before," Smith said.

"OK. And so if you don't believe everything in the newspapers, don't you think before you became a plaintiff in a lawsuit that you should have taken some personal action to verify whether things that were produced in a newspaper were really accurate?" Thompson asked.

Thompson berated Smith for not attending school board meetings. He implied that she might have other reasons for suing the district. He accused her of not listening to his questions and treated her like she was stupid. The woman's lawyers watched, irked, but also baffled. What was Thompson trying to accomplish with this overly aggressive line of questioning? Did he think this would win points with the judge?

Steve Stough glared at Thompson from a bench behind the attorneys. "This just got personal," he thought.

When it looked like Thompson was losing in the courtroom, he lobbied the public.

Parents' attorneys limited their media comments each day to a few frustratingly cautious statements before scooting off, dragging their wheeled briefcases behind them. But Thompson lingered on the courthouse steps, issuing grand pronouncements for the reporters and television cameras. Intelligent design, he told us, is a scientific theory based on empirical evidence, something he promised would become evident once the defense began to present its case.

He said no scientific theory should be judged on its religious roots. He reminded us that the Big Bang theory, when first postulated, was viewed as a religious proposition. We nodded our heads. It had become one of the defense's recurring themes. The Big Bang theory came up so frequently throughout the trial that Rothschild, joking, at one point asked a witness, "I won't ask you any questions about the Big Bang, and you won't answer any questions about the Big Bang. Can we agree to that?"

Despite his enthusiasm for the argument, I doubt Thompson believes in the Big Bang. The theory puts the origins of the universe at 13.7 billion years ago. Thompson espouses young earth creationism. He said on the courthouse steps, "I don't believe my ancestor was a monkey."

One could imagine that Thompson envisioned himself in the role of a modern-day William Jennings Bryan. Both believed evolutionary theory was responsible for contemporary society's ills.

However, their political views were quite different, and it's hard to imagine Thompson embracing much of what Bryan championed.

Thompson's argument, as he frequently stated it, is that evolution without the direct intervening hand of God removes the fear of eternal damnation, eliminating the consequences of sin. As fundamentalist Christians often say, "If children learn we came from animals, they'll behave like animals."

Bryan opposed evolution not because he believed it caused the masses to act like animals but because it allowed the wealthy to treat them that way. An ardent populist and three-time Democratic presidential nominee (he lost every election), Bryan believed that "social Darwinism" led to the exploitation of the working class and undermined democracy.

On some days, Thompson didn't show up at all. When I asked him about his frequent absences, he downplayed the importance of what was happening in the courtroom. He chided me for my belief that Dover might be his most pressing issue and touted his success in other battles.

Long before the trial was over, Thompson seemed to have given up.

Barbara Forrest is a tiny, slender woman in her mid-forties with narrow shoulders and a sweet Southern demeanor, which she admits to playing up when necessary in certain situations. If she wore a wide-brimmed floppy hat, she'd easily pass for a member of the local garden club. Yet, she was the defense's most feared witness.

A Southeastern Louisiana University philosophy professor, Forrest was the co-author of the 2004 book *Creationism's Trojan Horse: The Wedge of Intelligent Design*, which connects a series of dots regarding the history of the intelligent design movement and creationism.

Under Rothschild's questioning, she painted a picture of intelligent design as a covert religious movement—one that presented itself as scientific to the media and mainstream public. Under the surface, she said, leaders plotted a revolution not only in science, but also of modern culture.

Forrest testified that intelligent design did not spring from Genesis. Rather, its inspiration came from the Gospel of St. John: "In the beginning was the Word, and the Word was with God, and the Word was God."

In repeated accounts, she outlined how intelligent design's founders wanted nothing less than to have their concept permeate religious, cultural, and political life. At the same time that they were presenting intelligent design as science, proponents were courting Christians and promoting creationist beliefs.

"Christ is never an addendum to a scientific theory, but always a completion," William Dembski, one of the movement's chief proponents, wrote in his book *Intelligent Design: The Bridge Between Science and Theology.*

Forrest testified about the Wedge Document, the internal memo in which the Discovery Institute outlined its public relations strategy to destroy materialism and affirm the idea that human beings are created in the image of God. Forrest read from the document: "Alongside a focus on influential opinion makers, we also seek to build up a popular base of support among our natural constituency, namely Christians. We will do this primarily through apologetics seminars."

When Rothschild's questioning turned to *Of Pandas and People*, NCSE's Nick Matzke sat in the front row, back straight, a huge grin on his face. The twenty-nine-year-old science geek's work in the trial remained mostly behind the scenes. This was his favorite moment.

Matzke knew that the Foundation for Thought and Ethics

originally published *Pandas* as a creation science textbook. While combing through files in NCSE's cluttered office, Matzke found an FTE newspaper advertisement from 1981 seeking authors for an "unbiased biology" textbook that would be "sensitively written to present both evolution and creation science." Indeed, Dean Kenyon, one of *Pandas'* authors, later submitted a brief in the *Aguillard* case on behalf of creation science. Matzke wondered if early drafts still existed and suggested to lawyers that it might be interesting to find out. As part of the discovery process, Rothschild subpoenaed all documents related to the book.

Realizing that the drafts would be damning, FTE fought the subpoenas. It also filed a motion requesting to join the lawsuit, stating that it had a financial stake in the outcome of the court decision. Jon Buell, the head of FTE, argued that if Jones ruled that intelligent design was religion, it would be "catastrophic" for book sales.

But FTE remained its own worst enemy. Even as Buell fought its case, he revealed FTE's religious intent. The subpoenaed documents included paperwork filed with the Internal Revenue Service that states that FTE's nonprofit mission is "promoting and publishing textbooks presenting a Christian perspective." After listening to the evidence, Jones ruled that a financial stake was not sufficient reason to join the First Amendment lawsuit.

In addition to the tax documents, plaintiffs' attorneys received thousands of subpoenaed pages of drafts of *Pandas and People* from 1983, 1986, and 1987, along with the final published editions from 1989 and 1993.

Matzke called the material the trial's "smoking gun."

In the months prior to the trial, Forrest, Rothschild, and Matzke pored over the documents, and a clear pattern emerged.

The early drafts predating the 1987 U.S. Supreme Court decision of *Edwards v. Aguillard*—in which creation science was deemed religious—contained the word "creationism." In later drafts, writers dropped "creationism" and replaced it with the phrase "intelligent design."

Just before the trial began, Matzke flew to Philadelphia to meet with the legal team. After the meeting, he headed back to his hotel room. With time on his hands, he cracked his laptop and searched all the versions for the number of times the words "creationism" and "intelligent design" were used. He found that the two 1987 drafts formed a rather neat line of demarcation. With almost surgical precision, *Pandas'* editors cut the word "creationism" from the second 1987 draft, which followed the *Aguillard* decision, and replaced it with "intelligent design." However, in one instance, their scalpel slipped. One of the evolving phrases, discovered by Forrest, mistakenly became "cdesign proponentsists." The legal team later joked they had discovered ID creationism's evolutionary "missing link."

That evening Matzke drew up a chart illustrating the evolution of the phrases. The next day he showed the damning illustration to attorneys.

In her testimony, Forrest read from a 1986 version, predating the *Aguillard* decision: "Creation means that the various forms of life began abruptly through the agency of an intelligent creator with their distinctive features already intact—fish with fins and scales, birds with feathers, beaks, and wings, etc."

Then she compared it to the 1989 and 1993 published versions: "Intelligent design means that various forms of life began abruptly through an intelligent agency, with their distinctive features already intact—fish with fins and scales, birds with feathers, beaks and wings, etc."

The word switch exposed intelligent design's creationist roots. As Americans United's Richard Katskee wrote of the word switch: "Intelligent design followed the Supreme Court's rejection of creation science as night follows day. . . . After the Supreme Court rejected the proffered expert opinions in *Aguillard* claiming that creation science is 'science,' Kenyon and FTE took their draft textbook . . . and, with all the elegance of a word processor's algorithm, replaced references to 'creationism' with the new label 'intelligent design.' "

Or as Argento put it, "in addition to committing sloppy scholarship, Forrest's testimony suggested they were lazy, too."

For defense lawyer Thompson, this was the most damaging testimony of the trial. Forrest proved that intelligent design was clearly a religious notion. Thompson jumped into his cross-examination, desperately trying to raise doubts about Forrest's credibility. He asked, "When did you become a card-carrying member of the ACLU?"

Argento, trying to stifle his laughter, let out a loud snort. Later, he speculated in his column that Thompson was trying to get Forrest to admit that she and her friends "watched snuff films while snacking on aborted fetuses."

Thompson's line of questioning was cut off before he could get there. "Are you aware that they hold, the ACLU holds that all legal prohibitions on the distribution of obscene material, including child pornography, are unconstitutional?" he asked. Rothschild hopped to his feet. "Objection, your honor," he said. "This has absolutely no relevance to Dr. Forrest's testimony. This is not the issue in this case."

Thompson's head whipped from Forrest to Rothschild. His back to the judge, he snapped, "It's as much as relevant as a lot of stuff that you put on in this case that had no connection at all with my clients."

Rothschild stared at the judge and smiled. Jones said, "First of all, Mr. Thompson, if you're going to argue the objection, you argue it to me, not Mr. Rothschild."

"I'm sorry, Your Honor," Thompson said. Jones sustained the objection.

As Thompson continued to attack Forrest's credibility, he raised questions about her religious beliefs. He asked her to explain her views as a secular humanist ("We reject efforts to denigrate human intelligence, to seek to explain the world in supernatural terms, and to look outside nature for salvation"). He asked her whether she believes in the supernatural (she doesn't) and whether she believes in the "immortality of the human soul" (she didn't answer, following Rothschild's objection to the question).

Forrest occasionally responded to one of Thompson's questions with an "um hum," allowing just a little bit of honey to drip into her testimony. But Forrest wasn't playing fragile; she just had no need for bluster. Thompson raised questions about her criticisms of intelligent design proponents, saying she was condemning a theory simply because it has religious implications. But Forrest was clear in her testimony that she was not saying intelligent design had religious implications. Intelligent design is, frankly, she stated, "something which is, in essence, religious itself."

Thompson fought Forrest's testimony so vehemently not so much because he didn't want Judge Jones to hear it, but because he didn't want it in the court record where it would be reviewed on appeal. Forrest's testimony exposed the insincerity of intelligent design. It revealed that its avowed secular purpose was the sort of sham Justice Brennan decried in his opinion in the *Aguillard* decision. It wasn't just the school board that was trying to pass off intelligent design as science—the entire movement was based on sleight of hand.

Pastor Rowand watched the questioning of Forrest from a front-row pew. Her answers made him angry. This woman was an atheist. From his point of view, this made her biased against religion. Forrest, he felt, was trying to force her beliefs on him. Of course,

Forrest and the plaintiffs were objecting to using the school board as a pulpit, but Rowand didn't see it that way. It was his religious duty to bring people to God, whether in church or school.

As the drama unfolded in the courtroom each day, camera-wielding reporters approached plaintiffs for quotes. As Cyndi Sneath left the courthouse one day, a reporter called out to her. The journalist had witnessed Sneath's testimony and wanted an interview. Sneath, who avoided the media glare, kept walking. "I'm with *Rolling Stone*," the reporter called out. Sneath didn't turn, but Barrie Callahan, walking at Sneath's side, whipped her head around. But Sneath, Callahan remembers thinking, was a Great Dane, while she was a toy poodle. "Cyndi, it's *Rolling Stone!*" she said, jumping around. Sneath never broke stride. But *Rolling Stone*'s allure was too great to play cool for a girl who went to college in the '70s. "I'm a plaintiff," Callahan said. "You can interview me!"

A few days later, early in the morning, the magazine's photographer showed up at the Callahans' house. Fred and Barrie posed in their sunroom, the perfect image of the staid, concerned middle-class couple. But they could barely suppress their giggles as the song played in their heads: " . . . the thrill that'll get you when you get your picture on the cover of the *Rolling Stone*."

When the national media ran out of plaintiffs and defendants, they ventured to Dover to gather local color. They cornered students in pizza shops and their parents in grocery store parking lots, asking them, "So why Dover?"

After a couple of hours of touring the area, they thought they could sum up why this was happening in Dover. They came back with detailed stories from students of muddin' and keg parties, of gun racks on pickup trucks and Confederate flags. Pastor Grove played into the media's search for rural stereotypes. At the local fire hall, the ardent creationist hosted a viewing one night of Kent Hovind's video, *Why Evolution Is Stupid*.

Hovind, also known as "Dr. Dino," argues that Noah fit the dinosaurs onto his ark because he only took babies, which therefore took up less space. He also claims that Man was larger then, so God's specified cubit dimensions, based on a man's arm from fingertip to elbow, would have been longer. So the ark was bigger and could accommodate more animals.

His arguments are so preposterous that other creationist leaders discount them. A year later, Hovind would be convicted of tax fraud and sentenced to ten years in prison.

But at the Dover fire hall that night, people embraced the video uncritically.

Burt Humburg, a thirty-year-old medical resident who looks strikingly like Clark Kent, waited his turn in the back of the room. Humburg came to the fire hall to reason with the group, to explain why Hovind's assertions were wrong. A former Pentecostal believer, who grew up tithing and speaking in tongues, he understood what motivates fundamentalist Christians. He wanted them to know of his spiritual journey, of how he learned that one can believe in both evolution and God. Humburg grew up in Kansas and attended a mega-church. As a boy, he believed Jews were going to hell and accepted the notion that the earth was six thousand years old.

When he left home for Kansas State University, he excelled in science. He loved genetics and cell biology. Teachers considered him gifted. Then, in his sophomore year, he studied evolution. For the first time, he saw how everything linked together. He sat in class overwhelmed, his head in his hands. His professor misunderstood. Thinking Humburg was confused, he tried to help him grasp the concepts. But it wasn't that Humburg didn't get it, it was that his whole world had just changed. The scales had fallen from his eyes.

Humburg's fascination with science led him to a career in medicine. He joined the leadership ranks of Kansas Citizens for Science, an organization that has twice fought attempts by pro–intelligent design supporters to rewrite his native state's science education standards. In June 2005, he moved to Hershey, near Harrisburg, to become a resident in internal medicine at Penn State's College of Medicine. Sitting through much of the Dover trial, he wore a tie depicting his connection to his ape-like ancestors.

But evolution didn't steal his faith. It made it stronger. Today, Humburg loves a God open to possibility, not the rigid "doler-out-of-smitings" God of his childhood. He talks excitedly about the Jesus he knows, the one, he said, who loves to "rock people's world" and challenges them to "love thy neighbor."

He came prepared, lugging a portable bookstand on which he balanced the copious notes he had scribbled as he watched the video. After it ended, Humburg stood up, ready to address the crowd. A woman shouted from across the room, "You were brainwashed in college."

Humburg heard her words and realized that his effort was pointless.

The days didn't end with the closing of the courthouse doors.

As the trial convened each day, attorneys on both sides went to prepare for the next day of testimony. Over takeout food containers and pizza boxes, the parents' lawyers and scientists gathered in Pepper Hamilton's spacious conference room overlooking the Susquehanna River. Thomas More lawyers, meanwhile, worked out of their hotel rooms.

The plaintiffs and defendants drove back to Dover to evenings filled with campaigning for the approaching election. They knocked on doors and distributed fliers. On weekends, Dover CARES held chicken barbecues and sold homemade brownies to raise money for billboards and newspaper advertising. Between court during the day and politicking at night, Pastor Rowand found he barely had time to write his Sunday sermons.

Occasionally, their dual campaigns led to confrontations. One Saturday morning, the Rehms and Kitzmiller gathered at Sneath's house to review election material. Sneath glanced out her window. She saw Rowand and Bonsell outside, knocking on doors on her street. Bryan Rehm, wearing his Dover CARES T-shirt, grabbed his video camera and followed them. Christy Rehm chased after her husband, intending to head off a confrontation. But she thought of the board members' accusations that Dover CARES were anti-religious, and she grew furious. Stomping up to Rowand, she asked, "Why do you get to speak for God?" She told Rowand that she was a Christian, that she and her husband had faith and attended church every Sunday. Rowand didn't want to hear it. He called her a liar. "You're one of those ideological Christians," he said, towering over the small woman. Both of them exhausted, Rehm and Rowand shouted at each other in the street.

Each fall, the Mt. Royal Assembly of God holds its annual revival. Sister Angie, a fire-and-brimstone traveling preacher, spends a week each year at the church, providing inspiration for world-weary souls. Sister Angie is from Hanover, a town less than thirty minutes away, but that doesn't make the event any less special.

The whitewashed cinderblock church sits just off Route 74, the main artery through Dover. Saying she was led by God, Sister Mabel started the Pentecostal church in 1947 when just seventeen years old. She still preaches today. Sister Mabel has dark hair shot with gray pulled back in a hairnet. She wears shapeless dresses and flat, sensible shoes and speaks in a slow, unsteady voice.

One day about a month into the trial, in search of fresh story ideas, I attended one of the services, joined by two national journalists. We slipped quietly into a wooden pew in the back, trying to remain unnoticed, keeping our notebooks hidden away.

The people here spoke with an honest and touching literalism. A man stood up and turned to face the congregation. Without a hint of self-consciousness, he described heaven as a place where the streets were lined with gold. He said that meant every house must be a palace, because surely God would not use gold to build streets and then expect us to live in simple homes.

A woman with thinning hair spoke of her mother and of how, she believes, God saved her before her death. Now she is in heaven, the woman said, waiting to be reunited some day with her daughter. God is now trying to save her own children, the woman said, before it is too late.

After songs sung from ancient hymnals, Sister Angie began preaching. In her early eighties, she moved with a bird-like energy, darting up and down the single church aisle. She spoke in a thick, rural York County accent—a manner of speech often mistaken as Southern. Her white hair was pulled back in a tight bun, and she wore a black dress that reached almost to her ankles. She spoke of being shaken—"literally" she said—over the mouth of hell, not once, not twice, but three times. Sister Angie punctuated her points by kicking her leg out in front of her, whirling in a circle, and speaking in tongues. "Usuma, balak, efire."

"You've got to go further with God," she said. She spoke of her faith, how she once held back. But nothing stops her now, she said. "I want to go further with God tonight!" She shouted, raising her arms over her head. "Hallelujah" and "Amen" the men and women in the pews shouted back.

Sister Angie spoke of lost souls, parched like the ground during a Texas drought.

I recognized part of myself in these people. They are the church ladies of my childhood, who ladled out chicken corn soup on hot August afternoons. They are my neighbors, who watched me grow up, who kept vigil over me and reported any of my behavioral infractions to my parents.

I thought of my father and of the speaking of tongues and the Mark of the Beast and his belief in Satan's presence. I wondered what the writers sitting next to me in this pew would think of Dean Lebo.

9

Forty Days

Professing themselves to be wise, they became fools.

—Romans 1:22

Perched on the stand, Dr. Michael Behe, a small man with a graying beard and large, round glasses, looked a tiny bit like a cheerful saw-whet owl. The first witness in the defense's case, Behe clearly enjoyed his own testimony. A Lehigh University biochemistry professor and the author of *Darwin's Black Box*, Behe is the brightest light of the intelligent design movement. He is a devout Roman Catholic and father of nine. He's also a local boy. Behe graduated from Trinity Catholic high school, near my father's radio station.

Under the questioning of Robert Muise, the Dover attorney who once shopped *Pandas* to a West Virginia school board, Behe launched into a lengthy discussion of the lac operon, the lactose metabolism system found in some types of bacteria. Behe spoke in a precise manner and used exhaustively complex terminology. He relied on a laser pointer, using its red dot to emphasize his words on the overhead screen. Muise had been looking forward to this part of the trial, to finally argue his side of the case. The lawyer was particularly excited about discussing the bacterial flagellum and its "irreducibly complex" nature. Each time another plaintiffs' expert presented strong evidence for evolutionary theory,

Muise amiably assured reporters they needn't worry. The defense had some fascinating science testimony ahead, too.

Muise is a retired Marine officer who served in the Persian Gulf War. Like Behe, he has nine children. His wife, God bless her, home schools all of them. Muise became interested in intelligent design, he says, after reading *Pandas*. He is enthusiastic and, it seems, sincere. He wears his hair in a side part and speaks with a native Boston accent.

During the trial, when Muise got flustered, he'd pause, put his hands on his hips, and frown for a moment while he collected his thoughts. As he questioned Behe about the lac operon, he wasn't flustered but impressed.

"This might be hard to explain," Behe said. "[A specific type of amino acids] are the only acceptable amino acids at those positions, or that all of the single based substitutions that might be on the pathway to other amino acid replacements at those sites, are so deleterious that they constitute a deep selective valley that have not been transversed in the two billion years since those proteins emerged from a common ancestor. Now, translated into—"

"Yes," Muise said. "Please, into English."

". . . more common language, that means that a very similar protein could only work if it became even more similar to the beta-galactosidase that it replaced, and if you then also knock out that EBG galactosidase, no other protein . . . was able to substitute for the beta galactosidase. So the bottom line, the bottom line is that the only thing demonstrated was that you can get tiny changes in preexisting systems, tiny changes in preexisting systems, which of course everybody already had admitted."

Behe's testimony continued like this for hours. Reporters, at first, valiantly tried to follow along. But as Behe continued, their hands, scribbling notes, gradually . . . slowed, one by one, and finally paused, hovered over notebooks, then, at last defeated, dropped. The writer next to me dozed. Utterly lost, the rest of us in the jury box began to giggle helplessly. Judge Jones kept his face studiously composed and ignored us. On the plaintiffs' side of the courtroom, the lawyers looked baffled. Matzke followed the argument, he claims, but that was only because he recognized it as a rehash of Behe's lectures over the past ten years. Walczak struggled to hold back laughter. Even Rothschild, who would be the one to question Behe about his assertions, looked about the courtroom, watching reactions, and stopped trying to pay attention. He reflected on the hours the plaintiffs' legal team had spent in conference rooms, working with scientists, carefully rehearsing testimony so that it would be understandable and engaging not only to Judge Jones but also to everyone in the room.

Rothschild wondered if even Muise had any idea what Behe was saying.

After Behe exhausted his repertoire on the lac operon, Muise turned to Judge Jones and said, "Your Honor, we're about to move into the blood clotting system, which is really complex."

"Really?" Jones said, facetiously. "We've certainly absorbed a lot, haven't we?"

"We certainly have, Your Honor," Muise gushed. "This is Biology 2."

Behe would say later say he found the experience "all rather exhilarating."

But that was before Muise sat down and Rothschild stood up. Under Rothschild's cross-examination, Behe's mood shifted. The big words he so cheerfully used no longer sounded so impressive when subjected to repeated questions. At one point Rothschild reminded Behe of the National Academy of Science's definition of a scientific theory: "A well-substantiated explanation of some aspect of the natural world that can incorporate facts, laws, inferences, and tested hypotheses."

Under that definition, Rothschild pointed out, intelligent design couldn't be a scientific theory.

Yes, well, Behe admitted, he didn't like that definition. That's
why he developed one of his own. Behe prefers to define a scientific theory as "a proposed explanation which focuses or points to
physical, observable data and logical inferences."

Under his definition, which is actually closer to the meaning of
"hypothesis," intelligent design could qualify as a scientific theory, Behe explained. Rothschild referred to Behe's trial deposition. "I asked you, 'Is astrology a theory under that definition?'
And you answered, 'Is astrology? It could be, yes.' Right?" Rothschild asked.

"That's correct," Behe conceded.

At the end of the day, Argento blocked my exit from the courtroom. Our editors, concerned that Argento and I were overlap-
ping our coverage, asked us to start divvying up key points of
testimony. Argento stared at me, a pleading expression on his
face.

"Please let me take astrology," he begged.

In his column the next day, Argento pointed out that, according to Behe's definition, "intelligent design is on par with a 15th-
century science. Sounds about right.

"Actually, that's not quite fair. It short-changes astrology. For
example, my personal horoscope for Tuesday said, 'Confusion
could be your middle name, but many other people feel confused too.'

"Nailed it."

As the cross-examination continued the next day, Walter Rothschild watched his son from a seat in the back of the courtroom.
In high school, Eric Rothschild had been, as he describes himself,
"fat and ugly." Today, he is in his late thirties and has taken off

the weight of his youth. He has lost much of his hair and keeps the rest shaved close, which at first, from a distance, makes him look older. But up close, he comes across as deceptively young. He has a quick, gap-toothed smile, an intensely expressive face, and a nervous energy that makes me think he's always just about to run away. Rothschild's father watched the cross-examination with pride, and, he admits, a bit of jealousy. A retired CIA agent, Walter Rothschild thought, this is the moment when the son surpasses the father.

As Rothschild kept firing questions, Judge Jones also watched, amazed. He would later call it "a textbook" cross-examination. He remembers thinking Rothschild had completely crawled into Behe's head, for under the attorney's chipper and relentless questioning, Behe's assertions dissolved, revealing the very nature of intelligent design as an airy confection, ultimately no more substantial or satisfying than cotton candy.

For instance, Rothschild challenged Behe's dismissal that the "scientific literature has no answers to the question of the origin of the immune system."

"I see no Darwinian explanation for such things," Behe said, arguing that the immune system must therefore be irreducibly complex.

Rothschild trudged to the witness stand, plopping down a number of peer-reviewed articles and stacks of thick books on the subject of the evolution of the immune system. As he approached, Rothschild couldn't help but sneak a brief peek at the reporters in the jury box.

After stepping back, Rothschild asked, "Now, these articles rebut your assertion that scientific literature has no answers on the origin of the vertebrate immune system?"

"No, they certainly do not," Behe said. "My answer, or my argument, is that the literature has no detailed rigorous explanations for how complex biochemical systems could arise by a random mutation and natural selection, and these articles do not address that."

"So these are not good enough?" Rothschild asked.

So Rothschild tried again. And again. He continued piling material onto the stand until the pile dwarfed the professor. By the time he was done, Rothschild had stacked up ten textbooks such as *Origin and Evolution of the Vertebrate Immune System* and fifty-eight articles from prestigious journals like *Science*, *Nature*, and *Molecular Cell*, all of them detailing research on the evolution of the immune system. Rothschild stared at Behe over the material. "Is your position today that these articles aren't good enough?" he asked.

Attorneys would later refer to it as the *Miracle on 34th Street* moment.

But there was a significant difference between this scene and the make-believe one in the movie. Judge Henry X. Harper, buried under the pile of letters, admitted that, yes, Santa Claus exists. Behe, however, ignored the overwhelming body of work before his eyes. He gazed over the pile and said he remained unaware of any evidence of work done "in a detailed, rigorous fashion" detailing "how immune systems or their irreducibly complex components could have arisen through natural selection and random mutation."

Then Rothschild turned his attention to what was really a pretty simple question. Just as natural selection and genetic mutations are two of the driving forces of evolution, Rothschild wanted to know, what made intelligent design work? Behe maintained, in his expert report and in *Darwin's Black Box*, that "intelligent design theory focuses exclusively on proposed mechanisms of how complex biological structures arose." He spells out that this is intelligent design's only claim. Anything else, such as the identity of the designer, is speculation.

So, Rothschild asked, just what are the proposed mechanisms?

Behe couldn't answer the question. Instead, he recited, "We can infer design from the purposeful arrangement of parts." Each time he repeated the phrase, he raised his hands in a double-OK sign.

Rothschild repeated Behe's words: "Intelligent design theory focuses exclusively on the proposed mechanism of how complex biological structures arose."

"Please describe the mechanism that intelligent design proposes for how complex biological structures arose," Rothschild asked again.

Behe mentioned the Big Bang, he mentioned complex biological structures, he mentioned explosive processes, but he didn't answer Rothschild's question.

"Back to my original question," Rothschild asked. "What is the mechanism that intelligent design proposes?"

"And I wonder, could—am I permitted to know what I replied to your question the first time?" Behe asked.

"I don't think I got a reply, so I'm asking you, you've made this claim here, 'Intelligent design theory focuses exclusively on the proposed mechanism of how complex biological structures arose.' And I want to know what is the mechanism that intelligent design proposes for how complex biological structures arose?" Rothschild asked.

"Again, it does not propose a mechanism in the sense of a step-by-step description of how those structures arose," Behe said. "But it can infer that in the mechanism, in the process by which these structures arose, an intelligent cause was involved."

"But it does not propose an actual mechanism?" Rothschild asked, refusing to let it go.

Behe could not name the mechanism because there was none. Behe's sole argument for intelligent design was, if it looks designed, it is designed.

Walczak watched, filled with two competing emotions. The absurdity of it all made him want to laugh. To him, Behe sounded like a character in a Monty Python skit. Walczak could practically hear John Cleese parroting, "Purposeful arrangement of parts. Purposeful arrangement of parts. Squawk!"

Forced to finally show their hand, intelligent design's proponents revealed their bluff. And that also made Walczak furious—an utter fraud perpetrated on this country. "This is such a waste of time," he thought.

As Argento declared it, "It's the argument of an eight-year-old."

In his article "A Response to Critics of *Darwin's Black Box*," first published on the Discovery Institute's website, Behe wrote that intelligent design is "less plausible to those for whom God's existence is in question and is much less plausible for those who deny God's existence."

After referring to the article, Rothschild asked, "That's a God-friendly theory, Mr. Behe. Isn't it?"

Behe, as a Christian, argued that he was speaking from a philosophical view, much as Oxford University scientist Richard Dawkins was when he said Darwin's theory made it possible to be "an intellectually fulfilled atheist."

And then Behe said, "Arguing from the scientific data only takes you so far."

It wasn't just that its supporters—everyone from Dover's school board to the Discovery Institute—were lying. Intelligent design's entire premise is a lie, nothing but a bait-and-switch fraud. They promised scientific proof. But in the end, Behe said all they had was faith that what they were espousing was true.

At one point during the lengthy exchange, Rothschild asked whether the designer made every flagella or just "the first lucky one."

Behe said just the first one. Rothschild then wanted to know if the designer designed the mutations in the flagella that followed. "The proper answer is, we don't know," Behe said.

Because intelligent design proponents argue that one of the weaknesses of evolutionary theory is that it cannot be observed, Rothschild asked if intelligent design is observable. Behe said it is.

Rothschild asked Behe if he had witnessed newly designed structures appearing in the past five years. Behe said the designed structures that he's written about are much older. Rothschild asked if it was true that the intelligent designer might not actually exist any longer, that he could be, in fact, dead. Behe agreed that was true.

Rothschild paused. In a softer voice, he asked, "Is that what you want to teach school students, Dr. Behe?"

At the conclusion of trial that day, I walked to my car with a reporter from the German newspaper *Die Zeit.* The man, a large, intimidating German, exuberantly launched into a reenactment of the Behe cross examination as we waited for the parking garage elevator. He interpreted Behe as an antelope and Rothschild as a lion. The man stomped in a circle, pretending to be the lion taking little tiny nips out of the struggling prey, over and over again, he said, "until the antelope collapses exhausted." He loomed menacingly, inches from my face. I was half afraid he was going to bite me. But he drew back and placed his hands on his hips. "And then," he said in his thick German accent, shaking his head in nothing short of awed respect, "Rothschild attacks."

After trial each day, I'd go back to the *York Daily Record* newsroom and write a story for the next day. This particular night I wrote as my lede, "One of intelligent design's leading experts could not identify the driving force behind the concept."

I wrote that Behe said that "intelligent design theory focuses exclusively on proposed mechanisms of how complex biological structures arose. But during cross-examination Tuesday, when plaintiffs' attorney Eric Rothschild asked Behe to identify those mechanisms, he couldn't. When pressed, Behe said intelligent design does not propose a step-by-step mechanism, but one can still infer intelligent cause was involved by the 'purposeful arrangement of parts.'"

At about 11 P.M., I was gathering my things to leave the office, when Randy Parker, the managing editor, called. He wanted me to rewrite the story in order to make it appear more favorable to the pro–intelligent design side. He told me he thought my coverage had been "OK so far, but now I think we're just piling on."

I said that would be misrepresenting the truth. "They [the defense] must have done something you could lead with," he said. The editors had long been concerned with my reporting on the case, fearing the newspaper would offend fundamentalist readers. They encouraged me to write stories evaluating the holes in evolutionary theory. They reminded me of my obligation "to be fair and balanced," even as it became more obvious that there was nothing balanced about this debate. But until this phone call, no one had actively tried to force me to spin the story to favor a lie. Parker, who hadn't spent one minute in the courtroom, was trying to impose a false notion of balance on my coverage. I could hear my voice, shrill, say into the phone, "No, they did nothing. Rothschild eviscerated them."

Finally, Parker backed down. The lede stayed the same. When I left the office, I was shaking.

I thought of this notion of "fair and balanced" journalism and of how, somewhere along the line, we as journalists have gotten confused by a misguided notion of objectivity. It is our job to inform readers of the truth, not just regurgitate lies, even if it means the stories are no longer "balanced." Every day, I watched what took place in the courtroom. And while I didn't always get everything exactly right, this much I knew: If I went back to the newsroom and, in the interest of objectivity, pulled from my notes the best quote from the parents' attorneys and the best quote from Dover's attorneys and used them to present intelligent design and evolution as evenly balanced, then I'd be misleading readers.

Walter Williams, the first dean of the Missouri School of Journalism, wrote the Journalist's Creed. One century later, his words remain one of the strongest summations of the guiding principles of our craft, beginning with the simple declarative sentence: "I believe in the profession of journalism."

A few weeks after this night, I journeyed across the country, visiting museums dedicated to creationist views. I stopped in Columbia, Missouri, to visit a friend, who showed me these words dedicated on a bronze plaque outside the journalism school. I wish I had known of the creed that night while I argued with my editor, because in my inarticulate rambling, I was trying to convey what it expresses so succinctly: "I believe that the public journal is a public trust; that all connected with it are, to the full measure of their responsibility, trustees for the public; that acceptance of a lesser service than the public service is betrayal of this trust."

Williams also wrote, "I believe that a journalist should write only what he holds in his heart to be true."

With a week left to go in the trial, Bernhard-Bubb and Maldonado were finally able to defend their integrity. It was too bad they were unable to face their accusers. Neither Bonsell nor Buckingham sat in court when they testified. Walczak, who first questioned the reporters, had called newspaper accounts of what was said at Dover's board meetings "frankly, the best historical record we have." Walczak read their stories, line by line and quote by quote. He asked them to confirm that what they had written was accurate. They assured him, yes, their stories were correct. In searching for a new biology book, board members spoke of creationism. And in the six months between the meetings and the depositions, in which board members denied the remarks attributed to them, no one had asked the reporters to run a correction in their newspapers.

Thomas More attorney Ed White tried to discredit them in his cross-examination, and those of us in the jury box watched and held our breath as he did his best to cast doubt on their journalistic integrity. But Maldonado and Bernhard-Bubb never wavered. After a year of suffering board members' false recriminations, vindication arrived with their calm, unshakeable assertion of truth.

White accused Bernhard-Bubb of "misrepresenting" what took place. He asked her if she might have missed something while she was, perhaps, in the bathroom. He repeatedly raised questions about the accuracy of her quotes. "You didn't verify the accuracy of any quotes with the people you quoted in this article, correct, after you—or before you drafted the article?" he asked. In a composed voice, she said, "I didn't need to. I heard them say the things they said."

When it was Maldonado's turn, White questioned his qualifications. "Mr. Maldonado, your primary occupation is running the sandwich shop?" he asked.

"It's pretty much a tie between my writing and running the sandwich shop," Maldonado said.

"And you're—you don't have any formal journalism training though, correct?" White asked. "No, sir," Maldonado said. Like Bernhard-Bubb, Maldonado confidently said his stories were true.

"Are those people under oath when you're speaking to them?" White asked him.

"Do I make them raise their hand and swear on the Bible to tell me the truth, the whole truth, and nothing but the truth?" Maldonado said. "No, I don't do that . . . if that is your definition of being under oath." But, Maldonado said, he certainly hoped that when people speak to him, they tell the truth.

Out-of-town reporters eagerly awaited Buckingham's first appearance in court. Based on what they had heard of his past behavior, they expected fireworks. But the tired man who took the stand that day exhibited little of the bluster and retired-cop confidence he had demonstrated at school board meetings when he talked about standing up for Jesus and "liberals in black robes" taking away freedom. He limped into the courthouse with a cane and the assistance of his granddaughter. He seemed to have shrunk since I last saw him. The sleeves of his oversized tan sports coat hung down over his knuckles. But he still wore his trademark lapel pin of an American flag in the shape of a cross.

Plaintiffs' attorney Steve Harvey questioned Buckingham. While Harvey is typically warm and outgoing, he can also be intimidating, with his white hair and ice-blue eyes. Michelle Starr, a reporter at the *Daily Record* who covered the trial along with Argento and me, said Harvey reminded her of a white-tipped reef shark.

Harvey questioned Buckingham about his claim that he was unaware that newspaper articles reported that he had talked about creationism at public meetings. Buckingham said he stopped reading the newspapers because the reporters lied.

Harvey asked him about the article Bernhard-Bubb wrote for the *York Dispatch* in which she quoted Buckingham as saying, "Nearly two thousand years ago someone died on a cross for us. Shouldn't we have the courage to stand up for him?"

"And that's referring to you?" Harvey asked. "It's your, you claim that this article is just wrong about this, isn't that right?"

"That's right," Buckingham said.

"The reporter was just making it up?" Harvey asked. "That's your testimony?"

"I'm saying I didn't say it then," Buckingham said.

"The reporter was just making it up," Harvey pressed. "Isn't that what you told us earlier?"

"I didn't read the whole article, but if you're saying I said it then, if she's saying I said it then, yes," Buckingham said. His denials continued. Finally, Harvey played the Fox News videotape that had caused me to jump up and down nine months earlier. On a wide screen for everyone in the courtroom to see, Buckingham said, on camera, "We're just looking for a textbook that balances the teaching of evolution with something else, like creationism."

There was a pause as we waited to hear what Buckingham would say. "That was you speaking, wasn't it?" Harvey finally asked.

"It certainly was," Buckingham said.

Harvey continued, trying to elicit from Buckingham, with all the evidence in front of him, that he had indeed talked about creationism. But Buckingham's willingness to deny was undaunted. "Now, that's basically the same statement that was reported in the newspapers, isn't it?" Harvey asked.

"Pretty close," Buckingham said.

"And at first you told us you couldn't remember making that statement?" Harvey asked.

"Excuse me, when you first talked about that, I forgot about the interview," Buckingham said. "And what happened was when I was walking from my car to the building, here's this lady and here's a cameraman, and I had on my mind all the newspaper articles saying we were talking about creationism, and I had it in my mind to make sure, make double sure nobody talks about creationism, we're talking intelligent design. I had it on my mind, I was like a deer in the headlights of a car, and I misspoke. Pure and simple, I made a human mistake."

Harvey figured Buckingham would blame his OxyContin addiction. Instead, he blamed newspapers he claimed he didn't read for making him say something he insisted he never said.

Jenn Sherlock, the Fox News reporter who had interviewed Buckingham, watched from the jury box with the other reporters. After Buckingham finished his testimony, Sherlock laughed and shook her head. She had called him and set up the interview ahead of time. He had been happy to talk to her. She never ambushed him.

Next Harvey questioned Buckingham about his insistence that he didn't know anything about an anonymous donation of sixty copies of *Pandas and People* to the school district. In his January deposition, Buckingham repeatedly said he didn't know who donated the books.

But in court, Harvey produced an $850 check written out to Donald Bonsell, Alan's father, from Buckingham's checking account. Buckingham had signed the check, which was dated October 4, 2004. On the subject line of the check, he wrote, *"Pandas and People books."* Buckingham handed Alan Bonsell the check, who turned it over to his father. Donald Bonsell bought the books.

Buckingham explained that after his efforts to get the school board to buy *Pandas* failed, he went to his church, Harmony Grove, for help. "I said there is a need, if you want to donate that's fine," Buckingham told Harvey. "There is a need." Buckingham specified that he never "asked" for money from the congregation. Rather, he described a scene in which he stood up before the service and merely told parishioners that the district was looking for money. Members of the congregation stuffed envelopes with cash and one check and put them in a box at the back of the church.

Buckingham testified that he took the $850 raised and put it into his bank account.

Harvey read from Buckingham's deposition, in which he repeatedly said he didn't know where the books came from. "You have no idea?" Harvey had asked him. "I have thoughts, but I don't know," Buckingham had said.

As Harvey read his words back to him, Buckingham fidgeted. His cane kept getting stuck in a crack in the witness stand. Buckingham found it distracting. But everyone else in the courtroom seemed focused on the one point Harvey was driving home. Buckingham tried to hide the source of the money because it revealed his religious motivations.

Finally, Harvey stopped reading and glared. "Mr. Buckingham, you lied to me . . . isn't that true?"

"How so?" Buckingham said.

"By not telling me you took a collection," Harvey said.

"I did not take a collection," Buckingham said.

Buckingham never got a chance to articulate what he believed was the real point of the case. Before he left his hotel for court that morning, Buckingham had tucked a copy of the U.S. Constitution inside the breast pocket of his jacket. Had he been asked, he was prepared to read from it. In his day, he prayed from the Bible in school. Nowhere in the First Amendment are the words, "separation of church and state." In his mind, the entire case was based on a myth.

However, Harvey wasn't interested in discussing Buckingham's views on constitutional law. He wanted Buckingham to admit that he had lied. But despite the preponderance of evidence, Buckingham refused to concede.

"I thought I answered the question the way you asked it," Buckingham said. "Money was given to Alan Bonsell to forward to someone, turning out to be his father, that it was going to go someplace else. I don't . . . ."

Judge Jones, his jaw clenched, finally stopped the exchange. "Mr. Harvey, why don't you move to the next area. I get the point, and you've made the point very effectively, and I don't think you need to stay in this area. I'll give you some more latitude if you want, a little bit, but—"

"Your honor, I'm done," Harvey said.

"I get the point effectively," Jones repeated.

Later, outside the courthouse, Dover lawyer Richard Thompson stood before the cameras and said his client hadn't lied and that the case was going well. He said, "I don't think it was damaging at all."

But Steve Stough, who had watched Buckingham's testimony, knew differently. No matter how much Thompson might argue otherwise, he wasn't going to be able to clean up the obvious facts of the case. Board members lied. "You can't shine mud," Stough said.

When their turns came, the women on the school board testified that Buckingham and Bonsell had assured them that intelligent design was science. They said that was all they needed to know. It was clear they didn't have even a rudimentary idea about either evolutionary theory or intelligent design. Jane Cleaver, who once submitted a petition to institute school prayer, admitted that she knew nothing about science. But she believed it would be good to make students aware of what she repeatedly referred to as "intelligence" design. "I just feel that there's other theories out there that, we have the greatest science in the world right here in our nation," she said.

Heather Geesey, after admitting she ignored teachers' concerns, could only say, "Alan and Bill said it was a scientific theory."

Sheila Harkins, who once publicly attacked Maldonado's integrity, still could not provide a definition of intelligent design.

"You didn't really know anything about intelligent design, except that the two words existed side-by-side, isn't that right?" asked Tom Schmidt, the Pepper Hamilton attorney who cross-examined her.

"No, that's not true, huh-uh," Harkins said. "I knew a little bit, but I still don't know enough that I could ever teach it, no. I know very little still."

"Isn't it true that you didn't have a way to define or describe intelligent design?" Schmidt asked. "I still don't today," she said.

"And yet you're prepared to make that part of the curriculum at Dover Area School District, isn't that right?" Schmidt asked.

"And I think I've always said, you make them aware of it," Harkins said. "They find out for themselves." In the end, they weren't even able to answer the most basic questions about the issue they had so passionately embraced.

I wish I believed that those who confidently marched Dover into a federal courtroom represented a rare and isolated breed of American, that what happened could only have played out in Dover. But the truth is, this could have happened just about anywhere.

My father, the man who once shined a flashlight at the stars and taught his daughter to dream of infinity, believed only what he had been told in the tight-knit world of Christian evangelicals. Dover's school board was on the side of God. Nothing else mattered.

Heather Geesey testified that even though she had written a June 2004 letter to the newspaper defending the teaching of creationism, she didn't mean to convey that the board was considering teaching creationism. Rather, she said, they were considering intelligent design.

"You can teach creationism without its being Christianity,"

Geesey wrote in a June 27 letter to the editor that appeared in the *York Daily Record*. Nowhere in the letter did she mention intelligent design. Geesey, who giggled through much of her testimony, told the court that meant board members were actually talking about intelligent design and not creationism, despite what the newspapers had reported.

In her deposition before the trial, she said she didn't remember when board members had first discussed the concept publicly. But in her testimony in court, she said the letter helped jog her memory that they had indeed been discussing intelligent design at the June meetings. I can say with a great deal of confidence that nobody in the courtroom followed this bit of logic.

Judge Jones stopped her. "I have a question before you step down, Mrs. Geesey, because I'm confused," he said. "So am I," Geesey said laughing.

"Well, it's more important that I'm not confused than you're not confused," Jones said. "What . . . leads you to believe that intelligent design was discussed at the June meeting? . . . What? Point me to what in the letter, not generally, but specifically."

"That I thought . . ." Geesey said.

"I asked you that question because I don't see the words 'intelligent design,'" Jones said.

"Right. The part where it says, 'what we are doing.' I—since all the meetings run together, I didn't realize back then that I knew everything that was going on because it's not my committee," Geesey said cheerfully. "But by me saying that what we were doing was to choose a book that teaches the most prevalent theories, I mean that—that's what I was talking about."

Jones considered the fact that Geesey had no idea of the seriousness of her situation. A federal judge was questioning her to determine whether she had lied under oath. Geesey seemed to believe that they were simply having a pleasant conversation.

It didn't escape Judge Jones's notice that Alan Bonsell, the man who led his school district into a national First Amendment test case, frequently walked in late each morning, after testimony had started. Bonsell would take a seat in the front row and watch the proceedings with an amused, confident smile, his outstretched arms resting on the back of the pew. At the end of the day, he stood outside on the courthouse steps and explained to the cameras that the newspaper reporters were misrepresenting what was playing out in the courtroom.

Bonsell took the witness stand with the same sense of confidence and righteousness he exhibited throughout the trial. His attorney, Patrick Gillen, asked him, "Is your grievance or your complaint about the accuracy of the reporting something that is limited to the reporting of this incident, or more broadly?"

Chewing gum, Bonsell swiveled his chair to face Jones: "This is another thing that the court needs to know," he said. "This has been going on since before I was ever on the board. The two years that I was involved before I ran for the board in 2001 and ever since then, you know, just it came to a point where you couldn't trust what was said. I'm not saying every single word was wrong. I'm just saying it came to a point where it wasn't a trustworthy piece, it wasn't a trustworthy document to look at and see, and I heard it all the time from people all over the place, other board members from different school districts."

As Bonsell looked at the judge, Jones held his gaze, his expression neutral.

Under Gillen's questioning, Bonsell, speaking in a leisurely drawl, meandered through his testimony, talking about Dover's great accomplishments (no tax increase the previous year) and his personal commitment to improving education.

But during cross-examination, Steve Harvey got right to the point. While he usually writes across the top of his notes a reminder to slow down, this time Harvey didn't heed his own advice. Instead, he handed Bonsell a copy of his deposition and, without so much as a "Good afternoon," began to fire questions at him.

". . . When Mr. Rothschild at that deposition asked you about the donation of the books to the school district, you didn't tell him that you had received any check from Mr. Buckingham, did you?" Harvey asked.

"I don't believe so," Bonsell said.

"And you didn't tell him that you had a conversation with Mr. Buckingham on that subject, did you?" Harvey asked.

"That I had a conversation with him?" Bonsell repeated.

"Yes, that you spoke—that you spoke to Mr. Buckingham about the donation of this check?" Harvey asked again.

"I don't . . . I don't believe so," Bonsell said.

Barely pausing to breathe, Harvey read from the deposition:

Question: Are you aware that sixty copies of this book were donated to the school district?

Answer: Yes.

Question: Who donated those books to the school district?

Answer: I don't know.

Question: You don't know?

Answer: No, I don't. The question again?

Question: Who donated those books?

Answer: Who donated the books? They wanted to remain anonymous.

Question: Do you know who donated them?

Answer: Do I know the people that donated them?

Question: Yes.

Answer: I don't know—I don't know all the people that donated them, no.

Question: Do you know any of the people who donated them?

Answer: One.

Question: Who was that?

Answer: Donald Bonsell.

Question: Who is that?

Answer: He is my father.

Question: Do you know the names of anybody else who
donated these books?

Answer: No. . . .

Question: You don't know who the other people are?

Answer: I don't know who the other people are.

Harvey took a breath. "Was that your testimony on January the 3rd, 2005, Mr. Bonsell?" he asked.

"Yes, it was," Bonsell said.

"And you didn't mention anything to Mr. Rothschild about getting a donation, a check from Mr. Buckingham for $850, did you?" Harvey asked.

"No, I didn't," he said.

"And you understood that he was seeking that specific information, not that specific information, but that he asked you questions that should have called for that information, isn't that correct?" Harvey asked.

"No, I don't agree with that," Bonsell said.

The questioning continued at an exhausting pace, but Bonsell never conceded his dishonesty.

As Jones listened, his expression grew darker. At the conclusion of the day's testimony, he said he had a few questions of his own. He demanded to see the transcripts of Bonsell's deposition. Harvey offered to provide a clean copy—his version was marked with notes—later in chambers. "I want it now, if you have it," Jones said. "Hand it up."

As Jones reviewed the pages, his face grew red. Reporters,

parents, and lawyers glanced wide-eyed around the courtroom, awaiting the judge's response. Bonsell chewed his gum and swiveled in his chair, seemingly oblivious to the judge's rising ire.

Finally, Jones looked up. "When did you first become aware of the fact that your father was in possession of the $850 that was being donated to buy *Of Pandas and People*?" Jones asked.

"Well, Mr. Buckingham gave the check to me to pass to my father. He said this was money that he collected for donations to the book. So I gave it to him," Bonsell said.

"So you were the conduit . . . by which your father received the $850?" Jones said.

"Yes," Bonsell answered.

"Tell me why, in January of 2005, you didn't tell Mr. Rothschild on his repeated questioning that your—that Mr. Buckingham was involved in that exchange?" Jones demanded.

At first Bonsell glibly tried to dodge the question. "Basically because I understood the question to be, who donated the books? Do you know anybody that donated? I only knew my father was the one that donated the books. I am still to this day convinced, you know, that Mr. Buckingham didn't give any money towards the books," Bonsell said.

"He said to me, this is money that he collected towards the books. And I didn't ask him. You know, he didn't say—if he would have said, some of this money is mine, or I put 50 bucks in the pot, or I did this, I would have told Mr. Rothschild at that time."

Jones persisted. "The specific question was asked to you, sir: You have never spoken to anyone—anybody else who was involved with the donation? And your answer was, I don't know the other people. That didn't say, who donated? That said, who was involved with the donation?" Jones said, "Now you tell me why you didn't say Mr. Buckingham's name."

"Then I misspoke. Because I was still under—from behind—wait a second. I—well, I'm going back here—and so, yeah, that's my fault, Your Honor, because that's not—in that case, I would have—I should have said, Mr. Buckingham," Bonsell said.

Jones wanted to know why Bonsell didn't just let Buckingham buy the books, why Bonsell turned the check over to his father to make the purchase.

"He agreed to—he said that he would take it, I guess, off the table or whatever, because of seeing what was going on, and with Mrs. Callahan complaining at the board meetings, not using funds or whatever," Bonsell said.

After about fifteen minutes, Jones looked at the clock. He realized he needed to end his questioning. By the time he was done with him, Bonsell was flapping his hands and stammering.

The next day, when Bonsell returned to finish his testimony, he no longer chewed gum.

One Sunday near the end of the trial, I attended service at Pastor Rowand's church. What struck me the most was the difference in his demeanor. In the courtroom, he looked out of place and disconnected. But in church, he was alive, he laughed easily. After the service, he grabbed a giggling little boy and lifted him up over his head.

In church, Rowand was likable. That day, after the congregation departed, we sat on the stairs of the church, looking out into a soybean field turned gold with autumn, and we talked about what we believed and what we know to be fact.

Rowand told me of his father's fight against cancer. He far outlived doctors' predictions. For Rowand, his father's survival proves God's existence. While I didn't agree with Pastor Rowand's views on science, at least I understood his need for faith.

★ ★ ★

The night before the last day of trial, Matzke and Harvey remained at Pepper Hamilton's Harrisburg office, working until well past midnight, going over the final scientific testimony, reviewing, as they had many times in the past six weeks, issues related to the bacterial flagellum, molecular genetics, and macroevolution.

When they left to head back to their apartments almost two miles away, the night had slipped into dawn. Taxis were no longer running, and neither of them had a car. As they walked along the Susquehanna River, exhausted, their conversation drifted from science to religion. A passerby wished them, "Good morning."

Harvey, like Pastor Rowand, relies on faith that life has a purpose. But Harvey is more honest with himself. He understands doubt and believes that we can only try to believe in God. The next morning, nervous about the final hours of trial, Harvey paced outside the courthouse, smoking cigarettes and reciting the Lord's prayer, "Our Father, who art in heaven . . ."

As parents drove to court that morning, they were distracted by the knowledge that this would be their last day there. Over cereal that morning in their tiny apartment, Harvey had looked at Rothschild and said, "And I thought we were pretty good friends before we did this case." They all seemed to grasp that something special had taken place in the past six weeks, even if they didn't know yet what it was.

Many of the parents, who didn't know each other a year ago, had grown close. Cyndi Sneath and Tammy Kitzmiller planted a vegetable garden together. On summer evenings, they sat on their back porches and drank margaritas made with strawberries from their tiny patch. Bryan Rehm became the plaintiffs' soda-drinking designated driver and spent many nights shuttling his laughing wife and their new friends back and forth from the Racehorse Tavern.

Sneath and Callahan rode to court together each day, giggling and replaying scenes of exciting testimony and dramatic moments.

Just as they had grown fond of each other, they had become attached to the attorneys and the scientists. From the moment of their first press conference, frightened and not knowing what to expect, the parents clung to their legal team, just as they clung to each other. In turn, the lawyers, Rothschild and Walczak and Harvey and Richard Katskee and Tom Schmidt, looked out for them. That summer, the Kitzmillers, Sneaths, and Rehms vacationed together in North Carolina's Outer Banks. On the trip, they discovered a kitschy homemade spaceship rigged up in someone's front yard. Sneath commanded everyone, children and grownups, to get out of the car for a photo. As soon as they returned home, Sneath e-mailed the photo to their attorneys. The caption read, "We've discovered the intelligent designer!"

Together they learned about the archaeopteryx and whale ancestry, about man's evolution and the bacterial flagellum, about the legal process and First Amendment law. Teachers spoke of academic freedom and the desire to inspire students, just as Bertha Spahr once inspired Rob Eshbach to become a science teacher. Attorneys and scientists admired the parents, so committed to the Constitution and their children's education that they faced the judgment of their community. These people, who wouldn't otherwise have become friends, because of location or lifestyle, or even, yes, religious and political beliefs, were brought together in this courtroom. Now, they didn't want to let go of each other.

In his closing arguments, Dover attorney Patrick Gillen summed up the lawsuit by blaming Buckingham, saying it was "built on a molehill of statements by one board member fighting OxyContin addiction."

But Gillen portrayed Bonsell as a man motivated solely by a desire to improve education in his school district. He never feared the teaching of evolutionary theory, Gillen said, but only "science taught as dogma."

He argued that scientists are biased against intelligent design, but "the evidence shows that intelligent design is science, a theory advanced in terms of empirical evidence and technical knowledge proper to scientific and academic specialties. It is not religion."

It was the best Gillen had to offer. But Rothschild saw it differently. "What I am about to say is not easy to say, and there's no way to say it subtly. Many of the witnesses for the defendants did not tell the truth," he said in his closing remarks. "They did not tell the truth at their depositions, and they have not told the truth in this courtroom."

Rothschild reminded the courtroom of the human cost of their deception. "Two hardworking freelance reporters had their integrity impugned and were dragged into a legal case solely because the board members would not own up to what they had said."

He said what played out in Dover mimicked a broader movement. Both locally and nationally, he said, proponents discussed teaching creationism, later switched to the term "intelligent design" to carry out the same objective, and then pretended they had never talked about creationism. He said that intelligent design is not science but religion.

And he described the deep admiration he had for the eleven parents who were willing to stand up to their government, whose love and respect for their children was so great that "it spilled out of that witness stand and filled this courtroom.

"It's ironic that this case is being decided in Pennsylvania in a case brought by a plaintiff named Kitzmiller, a good Pennsylvania Dutch name. This colony was founded on religious liberty. For much of the eighteenth century, Pennsylvania was the only place under British rule where Catholics could legally worship in public.

"In his declaration of rights, William Penn stated, 'All men have a natural and indefeasible right to worship Almighty God according to the dictates of their own consciences. No man can of right be compelled to attend, erect, or support any place of worship or to maintain any ministry against his consent. No human authority can, in any case whatever, control or interfere with the rights of conscience, and no preference shall ever be given by law to any religious establishment or modes of worship.'"

The trial ended like a scene from a movie. Dover's attorney Patrick Gillen asked the final question: "Your Honor . . . By my reckoning, this is the fortieth day since the trial began and tonight will be the fortieth night, and I would like to know if you did that on purpose."

Jones paused, allowing a smile to cross his face. Even as the words were coming out of his mouth, he knew he'd never produce a better line: "Mr. Gillen, that is an interesting coincidence, but it was not by design."

People in the courtroom applauded.

As board members slipped out the back door of the courthouse to avoid the questions of the press, plaintiffs greeted the media enthusiastically.

Jones climbed into his car alone that night for the ninety-minute drive to his home in Pottsville. He pulled out of the parking lot, following the route that takes him in front of the courthouse. He could see the crush of cameras and microphones. At the center, he could make out the top of Rothschild's shiny head.

The scene made him a little sad. "Well, it's over," he thought. Jones caught himself wishing that he could grab a beer with the lawyers.

10

Seeking Comfort

Man of God, Man of God, that ain't the preachin' of a Man of God

—Eliza Gilkyson, "Man of God"

The trial ended on a Friday, four days before the school board's general election. The incumbents and their challengers spent the weekend knocking on doors and shaking hands. By Tuesday, the candidates on both sides and their supporters were exhausted. Terry Emig, a Dover CARES candidate, had lost his twenty-year-old daughter, Emily, a month earlier in a car accident. Emily, studying to be a teacher, was a big supporter of Dover CARES. Rather than drop out of the race, Emig campaigned through his grief. When Buckingham quit the school board that summer, he opened up another seat for the fall election. Eight candidates from each side competed for eight spots on the school board. Only one incumbent, Heather Geesey, was not up for election.

Bonsell wrote and mailed out a last-minute flyer linking opponents in Dover CARES to the North American Man/Boy Love Association. Since Bryan Rehm was both a candidate and a lawsuit plaintiff, it was a reference to the ACLU's free-speech defense of the organization, which lobbies for the removal of pedophilia laws, in a 2000 Massachusetts case. "I fear the ACLU more than I fear al-Qaeda," said Ron Short, one of the members of the school board running for election.

On Election Day, students, led by Tammy Kitzmiller's daughters Megan and Jess, and Christy Rehm's daughter Alix, gathered after school outside one of the busier voting precincts, holding up signs that said, "Honk if you're for Dover CARES." As I talked to the girls, a steady stream of cars passed by. Each time a car beeped its horn, the boys cheered and the girls jumped and squealed. A *New York Times* photographer snapped a photo of Megan holding up her sign.

Cyndi Sneath, who was smoking a cigarette outside Dover's library, said she hoped that Dover CARES candidates would eke out a majority, but she feared voters might be split. I chatted with Pastor Ed Rowand outside Dover's fire hall. He thought that maybe voters would split their votes, too. "What do you think?" he asked. I shrugged and told him honestly that I had no idea. Two college students, making a video documentary, hovered nearby. They had driven down from Boston for the election and asked to interview him. As I left, a Dover CARES candidate walked up. They interviewed him, too.

Stough worked the polls outside his church, Friendship United, just south of the borough. His cell phone rang throughout the day as he fielded calls from newspapers, including the *New York Times* and one from France.

Eric Riddle, one of the board members running for election, stood a few feet away, handing out pamphlets to voters as they approached.

Like Sneath, Stough just hoped they would win a majority. But throughout the day, Stough noticed something interesting. As people approached, Riddle handed them pamphlets. He'd point to Stough and tell them there stood the guy with the ACLU. Some of the voters walked up to Stough and told him not to worry. They wouldn't be voting for liars.

Stough had printed out the transcript of Judge Jones grilling Bonsell, but he found that most people didn't need to read it. As he and Sneath and other parents watched the deception that had taken place in the courtroom, they had thought, if only voters knew what we know. Standing outside his church, Stough started to think that maybe they did.

That night, after the polls closed, he stayed as election officials counted the results. The last one to phone in poll numbers, he read the results to Sneath, who double-checked them against her figures. Excited, she had Stough read them again.

"We got eight seats," she said. Dover CARES swept the election, routing the incumbents. Alan Bonsell and Sheila Harkins received the fewest number of votes.

Sneath told Stough to hurry to get up to the house where everyone was celebrating. He gathered up the election signs and jumped in his truck. By the time he arrived, everyone had heard the news. From a house on top of a hill overlooking Dover, the plaintiffs took phone calls from journalists from around the world. They listened for a few moments and handed their phones to the newly elected school board members.

Stough gave Bernie Reinking, who would become the board's president, his cell phone, parked himself next to the cooler, and drank a beer.

It's hard to know what precisely prompted residents' final votes. In the spring primary, they split their votes. What changed their minds? Stough figured that every time school board members opened their mouths, they cost themselves votes. Not much of a campaign strategy for Dover CARES, Stough admits, but "it worked to our advantage."

Perhaps Dover residents had grown weary of the debate and the media attention, weary of the comparisons to Dayton, Tennessee, and the Scopes Monkey Trial. Perhaps people who once resisted the attention of outsiders had grown tired of feeling like they had become a national joke.

Two days later, on his show *The 700 Club*, televangelist Pat Robertson issued his verdict: "I'd like to say to the good citizens of Dover: If there is a disaster in your area, don't turn to God. You just rejected him from your city."

Later in the day, he issued another statement saying he was simply trying to point out that "our spiritual actions have consequences."

"God is tolerant and loving," Robertson continued, "but we can't keep sticking our finger in his eye forever. If they have future problems in Dover, I recommend they call on Charles Darwin. Maybe he can help them."

In Dover, residents denounced the remarks. Church pastors said that Robertson doesn't speak for them or their community. The Reverend Warren Eshbach, who once warned board members that they would divide the community, urged residents to focus on more positive messages. "The community of Dover needs healing and we need to begin to work together," Eshbach said.

Even one of the ousted board members, David Napierskie, said Robertson went "too far."

"I mean, he's entitled to his opinion, but I don't think it's appropriate to label all of the people of Dover in that sense," Napierskie said. "Quite frankly, the Dover CARES people are entitled to their opinions . . . ."

Jeff Brown, who quit the school board along with his wife, Casey, over the intelligent design policy, said Robertson contradicted testimony.

"According to sworn testimony, intelligent design has nothing to do with God," he said. "Then Pat Robertson says if you don't support it, God will hate you. These clowns want it both ways. I have a zero tolerance for sanctimonious morons who try to scare people."[1]

The day after the Dover school board election, I climbed into my car for a two-week creationist-inspired road trip. Judge Jones had said he wouldn't be issuing his decision for at least four more weeks. I hoped to use that time to gain insight into fundamentalist beliefs. I planned to visit museums—and there are many of them—dedicated to the concept of creationism. I had read about these places before the trial and had become fascinated. I wanted to see them for myself.

My journey led me to Texas. Dinosaur Valley State Park in Glen Rose, Texas, sits in the Paluxy Flats, near the northern edge of the Hill Country. About 105 million years ago, the area perched at the edge of an ocean, an ancient seashore now turned to stone. According to park exhibits, fossilized dinosaur prints were made several days after a violent storm surged across the low-lying coastline, burying the marshes with sandy, limey mud. An exhibit offers this enticing narrative, "Across the still-wet surface, a small group of sauropods journeyed south in search of food, followed by their mortal enemies."

Yet at a place just outside the state park, they tell a much different story. The Creation Evidence Museum is housed in a single room of a double-wide trailer standing at the center of a flat open field of parched grass. Here, just as at other creationism museums, we learn that dinosaurs and man once frolicked together.

On the day I visited, founder and director Carl Baugh was not there. Instead, a videotape of him provided the only tour. People watched the movie from several rows of hard-edged seats lined up in front of the screen. Two dark-eyed boys about ten years old sat behind me. They watched blank-faced as Baugh explained the science of flood geology: "The voice of God, whether by direct vocal intervention or by indirect vibrational disruption, at microwave energy level penetrated the great water reservoir beneath the earth's granite crust," he said in the video.

Baugh is perhaps best known for his claim to have discovered human footprints inside dinosaur prints. He said he has excavated 11 dinosaurs, 475 dinosaur tracks, 86 human footprints, and 7 cat prints from the Cretaceous limestone along the Paluxy River. This proves, he said, that dinosaurs, humans, and cats all lived together. Also on display: the purported remains of a fossilized human finger; the famed Burdick Track (a 6½-by-14-inch footprint of a person which, according to the museum, belonged to a 7-foot-tall man); and a picture of a contemporary human giant.

The museum also boasts a hyperbaric chamber designed to recreate the atmospheric conditions of the Garden of Eden. The venom of a poisonous snake inside the chamber is changing into a nontoxic serum, Baugh said in the video. In the days before Original Sin, we are reminded, there was no death, and therefore, venom had no purpose in Eden. Later I peered into the chamber. It was empty. The woman behind the counter, who didn't seem to really want to chat, told me they were in the process of getting new snakes.

"So where do I find these human footprints?" I asked her. She told me they're on private property and the owner never lets people on the land any more because of vandalism. I was too bored to argue. The two boys left at the same time as I did. In the hour they were there, they never asked a question.

Later, I went back to the state park, where I sat on a large limestone rock next to a pool of quiet green water where a bend in the Paluxy River formed an old swimming hole. The sun shined warm on my head. If it had been fifteen degrees warmer, I would have taken off my jeans and slipped into the water. Two dragonflies performed a courtship dance in a pool of light, dipping and rising over the tension of the water's surface.

I looked at a flat, wide rock near the bank just a few inches under the water. There I saw the three-toed footprints of an Acrocanthosaurus, who passed through millions of years ago, perhaps hunting, when this was once a much different landscape of tidal flats and marsh. I stretched my fingers and imagined placing my hand in one of the prints, which were just out of reach of my dry perch.

In his final words in *The Origin of Species*, Charles Darwin wrote, "There is grandeur in this view of life. . . . From so simple a beginning endless forms most beautiful and most wonderful have been, and are being, evolved."

There is a story of Darwin collecting beetles as a young man. Excitedly, he found a terrific rare specimen, likely a bombardier beetle, and grabbed it with his hand. But before he could put it away, he saw another one and grabbed that one with his other hand. But then, he saw another one. Not wanting to release the two he already held, he stuck one in his mouth and held it between his teeth. "Alas!" he later wrote. "It ejected some intensely acrid fluid, which burnt my tongue so that I was forced to spit the beetle out, which was lost, as was the third one."[2]

I adore this image of Darwin—a man so excited by nature and so curious, so enraptured with the possibility of discovery that he shoved a beetle into his mouth without weighing the consequences.

After a five-year journey round the world on the HMS *Beagle*, Darwin returned home in 1836 with a collection of wildlife and the genesis of a truly revolutionary idea. A year after his return, he sketched the notion on which all of modern biology is based— a roughly drawn evolutionary tree, topped with the cautious caption, "I think."

Yet Darwin, painfully aware of religious objections to similar theories, was reluctant to publish his findings regarding natural selection. He loved his wife, Emma (although, in listing the pros and cons of marriage, he noted, "constant companion . . . better than a dog"), and some historians speculate that much of his reluctance to publish stemmed from Emma's strict Anglican beliefs. She feared his ideas would prevent them from meeting again in the afterlife.[3] It wasn't until another British naturalist, Alfred Russel Wallace, also stumbled onto the concept of natural selection that Darwin was moved to publish *The Origin of Species* in 1859.

What a terrible burden this must have been for Darwin. To grapple with such an amazing, elegant concept, yet be unable to share it with the woman he loved.

I thought of the boys back at the museum, and I wondered, would they see what I see? Would their imaginations let them travel back through time and picture these great beasts, stalking prey, passing through here? Would the boys want to wade curiously into the water and explore these prints? Or would they stay firmly on this rock, sitting impassively, distrustful, fearful of what this evidence tells them, reluctant to explore? Would they grow up to be like Alan Bonsell and my father, hating science because they've been taught that it means they must abandon their faith?

John Haught, a Georgetown University theology professor, testified during the trial that he thought it was a mistake to assume that one cannot believe in evolution and religion, that to argue otherwise presumes to know the mind of God.

"The God of intelligent design seems to be . . . a kind of tinkerer or meddler who makes ad hoc adjustments to the creation, whereas what I would want a child of mine to think when he or she thinks of God is something more generous, much more expansive, a God who can make a universe which is, from the start, resourceful enough to unfold from within itself in a natural way all the extravagant beauty and evolutionary diversity that, in fact, has happened.

"To put it very simply, a God who is able to make a universe that can somehow make itself is much more impressive religiously than a God who has to keep tinkering with the creation."

Throughout the trial, I thought I noticed a sadness in Tammy Kitzmiller's smile. She has never felt at home in Dover. Some have treated her with suspicion because she is a single mother. As the lead plaintiff in what so many viewed as a lawsuit to banish God, she's pretty sure that now she'll never fit in. Her teenage daughters will be on their own soon. She soon will be forty, and she thinks maybe she would like to sell everything, buy an RV, and drive around the country until she finds a place where she belongs.

But I wonder if she'll ever find such a place.

The sun was hanging low in the sky when I left the Texas park. I felt sad and lonely. I wanted to talk to someone about the dinosaur prints, someone who shared my excitement. But I was alone. When the trial ended, I felt abandoned by like-minded souls. I'm jealous of the scientists and lawyers who returned to their college campuses and high-rise office buildings, far away from well-meaning prayers and talk of salvation. What would it be like to go a week without being judged?

As dusk gave way to night, I continued driving, randomly, across these ancient tidal flats. An almost-full moon lit the sky. I felt as if I was searching for something. Still, as I had told my father a week before, I wasn't sure what that was. I had made it to Texas, but I was no farther along on my journey. On one of the side roads out of town, I passed a tattoo parlor. The lights were off, but a small red neon "Open" sign beckoned.

I thought of the Flying Spaghetti Monster. I thought, "Wouldn't it be kinda cool . . . ."

When members of the Kansas State School Board pushed to change the definition of science to include supernatural explanations, they were paving the way to have intelligent design taught alongside evolution. In response to their discussions, a concerned young man named Bobby Henderson wrote letters to board members in the summer of 2005. He agreed wholeheartedly that evolution was just a theory. But he also suggested that if the board wanted to present alternative theories, then it should also offer his personal version of life's creation—the Flying Spaghetti Monster.

According to Mr. Henderson's theory, which he assures us is based solely on empirical evidence, all life was created by the Flying Spaghetti Monster with the gentle touch of his noodly appendages. Henderson also claims that the science connecting man's behavior to global warming is bogus. Rather, he links the warming of Earth to the inverse relationship between the number of pirates on the high seas today. Also known as Pastafarianism, the Church of the Flying Spaghetti Monster claims to be the fastest-growing carbohydrate-based religion. Henderson's heaven includes a stripper factory and a beer volcano. Every Friday is a religious holiday. Also, and this is an interesting point, in the Church of the Flying Spaghetti Monster, zero people have been killed in His name.

I pulled into the tattoo shop's parking lot. Timidly, I stepped through the door.

Sweat poured off my face as I stretched out face down on a reclining chair. A woman with red hair tried to distract me. The new girlfriend of the shop's owner, she told me about her children and grandchildren, who were scattered across the country. I tried to follow the details, but all I could really focus on was the fact that a man was repeatedly jabbing a needle into a spot just above my butt.

And, well . . . it really . . . really stung. "Can we please stop for a minute?" I begged. The man laughed. Apparently, I was a sissy. It was my first tattoo. He told me he had never had anyone ask for artwork of a Flying Spaghetti Monster. This may be the first one in the world, I said. He nodded, picked up his needle. "Ready?" he asked. Break was over. As he resumed, he glanced back and forth between my skin and a picture that we had printed off the shop's computer.

The tattoo artist was probably in his mid-twenties. He had long, soft dark hair and a beautiful dimpled smile. Despite the jabbing, his hands were gentle. It occurred to me that I was probably revealing to him a less than flattering view of myself.

I tried to pick up my conversation with the woman. Through clenched teeth, I asked, "So, you say your son lives in Wisconsin?"

The woman offered me tequila. "Yes," I said, sincerely, "tequila would be great." She laughed. No tequila was produced. "So," she asked, "What is a Flying Spaghetti Monster?"

Wincing, I explained about the dinosaurs and the footprints, about Darwin and little boys and the hyperbaric chamber. I told her about the parents in Dover and the trial and the lies. I said I wanted to do something symbolic, to honor scientific inquiry and curiosity. I said, "It's my own little personal tribute."

When I left the tattoo parlor, my hip stung. It was not yet 9:30 at night, but Glen Rose looked asleep. As I drove back to my hotel, the moon shined on the open fields. I thought of the dinosaurs roaming this land. I still felt them out there, spirits lumbering just out of view. I wanted to reach out and touch one.

The next morning, I left Glen Rose and drove south through the Texas Hill Country. It was mid-November, but the sun was warm and shined on scraggly cedar, live oak, and little bluestem grass, turning the gently rolling landscape from brown to gold.

The Gourds, an Austin-based band of scattered influences, mixed politics, loopy lyrics, and whiplash nonsequiturs, were playing that night in the Hill Country town of Comfort. I knew nothing about Comfort, but when I arrived, it immediately felt like home.

Unknowingly, I had stumbled into a community of like-minded souls. Founded by German freethinkers, Comfort's citizens evidently weren't much into being told what to do. During the Civil War, it was the only town in Texas to support the Union. A plaque stands as tribute to a stubborn streak and a resistance to dogma. People were living in Comfort, the sign says, fifty years before anyone ever got the idea to build a church. Today, Comfort, which sits along the banks of Cypress Creek, is filled with wide streets and western-style storefronts. Along Main Street, cats curl up in the sunshine. In an ancient, dusty hardware store that marks the center of town, bait is kept in an old stand-up refrigerator, next to the milk and butter. Packs of rat traps sit on shelves next to canned corn, car parts next to antiques.

On the other side of town from the hardware store—about eight blocks—the band was playing outside, behind a bar boasting the oldest bowling alley in the state. The temperature had fallen with the sun. As I arrived, the musicians and a small collection of their fans huddled around a large bonfire, drinking beer and trying to stay warm. I bought a Shiner Bock and joined them.

Max Johnston is a native Texan with a sideways smile. He plays the fiddle, mandolin, banjo, and lap steel for the Gourds. His hair, since he cut it short, sticks out in all directions, and sometimes when he shaves, which is not often, he misses spots, and tufts of hair sprout from his face.

Johnston joined the group by the fire and asked me where I'd been. I told him I came from Glen Rose. He said that, as a boy, he used to play there in the swimming hole. His father, Dollar

Bill Johnston, a Dallas folk singer and unrepentant atheist, used to take him. Lifting a foot slightly off the ground, Johnston showed me how he used to place his foot in the dinosaur's prints, the same ones I sat beside a night ago. He was making idle conversation. But I was touched. I saw his little boy's foot stretching through time, connecting him to our collective human past.

Two days later, I woke up homesick in a seedy hotel in South Austin, Texas.

I threw my backpack and my laptop into the car and headed north for Dallas, then turned west for Texarkana. Son Volt's "Tear Stained Eye" played on the car CD player. "Can you deny, there's nothin' greater, nothing more than the traveling hands of time."

I started my drive in a T-shirt. The next morning, twenty-four hours later, I wore a coat as I passed the northern, snow-covered slope of Virginia's Clinch Mountain.

In the eighteenth and nineteenth centuries, the Scotch-Irish sailed across the Atlantic carrying their fiddles and settled in these Appalachia hills. They brought with them their own Celtic tunes, but like everything else in this country, their music evolved, changing into something possessing a uniquely American imprint. These hills gave birth to country and bluegrass music, collected songs of faith written by a people who had little else. There is an old-time song that goes, "Gathering flowers for the master's bouquet, beautiful flowers that will never decay, gathered by angels and carried away, forever to bloom in the master's bouquet."

I thought of mothers pacing with croupy babies in Appalachia kitchens, praying, please God, let this child make it through the winter. These people had to hold onto something—even if it's just the belief that their dead babies might someday be flowers.

We're never going to fix this. The religious fundamentalists have shackled themselves, and us, to this notion of heaven and hell. In trying to escape the fear of their own mortality, they have merely replaced one hell with another.

As a baby, I'm told, I fought sleep. I'd cry and cry, but I refused to close my eyes. My father would stretch out on the couch and rest me on his chest. He rubbed my tiny back over and over again, singing to me the same song until I finally drifted off. "Down in the valley, the valley so low. Hang your head over. Hear the wind blow." His baritone voice was the only thing that comforted me.

This past year, I watched my father grow tired and age. We have begged him to see a doctor, but he refuses. He believes only in healing by faith. He tells us he is ready for the next life. But even as he says this, we can see that he is afraid. I'm sure much of this is because my father fears that his wife and children do not believe in God. That we are not saved. And so, he believes we are going to hell.

My father will leave this world believing he will never again wrap his arms around his daughter, that despite eternal life (eternity? Oh God, what a concept), we will never be reunited. Rather, he believes that I will exist in a place "where their worm dieth not, and the fire is not quenched."

If you believe this, truly believe this, then how could anything else matter? The First Amendment, scientific reality, the truth? All this would mean nothing. I grasped this. And for those of us who don't believe, can't believe, we have to bear the weight of this fear.

I am so sorry I can no longer give him this reassurance that I believe, that I can be saved. I am unable to give my father the one thing I know would comfort him.

And because I can't, we torture each other. I am only a few miles from home, and I still don't understand where these ideas come from. I've searched for answers and found none. Would I accept heaven, if I knew it meant my loved ones are doomed to hell?

I don't think so. But maybe, just as I don't have a choice in whether I can accept this faith, my father doesn't have a choice, either.

But this is not just about my father and me, or Alan Bonsell and Cyndi Sneath and the town of Dover. This is about this country. The believers and the nonbelievers. Will this dividing line of religious fundamentalism always be there and always separate us—like a fault running through our hearts? Tectonic plates shift, sometimes drifting far apart, sometimes clashing against each other, perhaps, but they will never be joined.

I pulled into my driveway thirty-six hours after leaving Austin. I sprawled in a chair, tipping back a Pennsylvania-brewed Yuengling lager. I was glad to be back home, back in York County. My husband Jeff mentioned that the Christians came to our house while I was gone. They knocked, but no one was home. They left pamphlets at our door, warning us that we are going to hell.

11

"Breathtaking Inanity"

The job before democracy is to get rid of such canaille. If it fails, they will devour it.

—*H. L. Mencken*

Judge Jones thumbed through the verdict one more time. He had been working on the document for five weeks, ever since the trial ended. Yet, each time he picked through it, he found another grammatical error, another typo. He threw it down on his desk. He couldn't look at it anymore.

Go ahead, he told his law clerk. File the document.

At Pepper Hamilton's Harrisburg office, the lawyers wandered in and out of their offices, drinking coffee, chatting distractedly with the scientists, Kevin Padian and Eugenie Scott, who had both flown in for the decision. Empty potato-chip bags and candy wrappers littered Rothschild's makeshift office, the result of nervous nibbling in the past few months. Someone started a pool on what time Jones would issue the verdict.

The plaintiffs and teachers, meanwhile, tried to go about their daily routines, unable to focus.

Just as she promised the year before, Bertha Spahr had made her chocolate biscotti for her teachers just in time for the decision. Spahr wasn't the only one to distract herself in the kitchen. Barrie Callahan baked Christmas cookies. Steve Stough spent the morning in class, sneaking peeks every few minutes at his e-mail. Finally, agitated by the fact he still hadn't heard anything, he jumped in his truck and drove home. On the way, he called Cyndi Sneath. Just climbing out of the shower, Sneath lunged for the ringing phone. "What have you heard?" Stough wanted to know.

Just after 10:30 that morning, the verdict filed moments earlier, Jones turned on the television in his chambers and waited. In fifteen minutes, the headline scrawls began. The stories soon followed. His law clerk, Adele Neiburg, and his deputy, Liz O'Donnell, watched with their boss. They flipped through the channels—CNN, MSNBC, Fox News. Jones's picture kept popping up on the screen. The two women turned from the television and stared at him.

With Stough on the phone, Sneath glanced at her television. She saw the CNN scrawl. "It's coming across the bottom," she told him. "Judge issues decision in Dover."

As Callahan glanced out the window, her phone rang. She panicked. An NBC news crew was walking up the front steps to her house. She had cookies in the oven, and she didn't yet know if the news was good or bad.

The e-mail showed up on computers at Pepper Hamilton. Lawyers hit print and grabbed copies. At first, there was little sound except for the flipping of pages. Padian started reading from the beginning. Lawyers jumped to the end, where they knew the ruling would be:

"Defendants' ID Policy violates the Establishment Clause of the First Amendment of the Constitution of the United States. . . . Defendants are permanently enjoined from maintaining the ID Policy in any school within the Dover Area School District."

It was better than they hoped.

"The breathtaking inanity of the Board's decision is evident when considered against the factual backdrop, which has now been fully revealed through this trial. The students, parents, and teachers of the Dover Area School District deserved better than to be dragged into this legal maelstrom, with its resulting utter waste of monetary and personal resources."

Rothschild darted through the office, reading aloud from the decision. Walczak called Ken Miller. Riding on a train, the scientist could only make out Walczak's hoarse voice screeching, "Grand slam! Grand slam!"

For in 139 pages, Jones not only chided what he described as school board members' "breathtaking inanity," he also ruled that intelligent design was not science.

While the parents and attorneys thought that Jones might rule in their favor regarding the board members' obvious religious motivations, the bigger question had always been whether he would take a position on ID as science. His verdict determined that it was unconstitutional to teach the concept in science class.

"It is our view that a reasonable, objective observer would, after reviewing both the voluminous record in this case, and our narrative, reach the inescapable conclusion that ID is an interesting theological argument, but that it is not science," Jones wrote.

He concluded not only that it was indeed a religious proposition, but that when its supporters spoke of "the designer," they were talking about a specific deity: "The writings of leading I.D. proponents reveal that the designer postulated by their argument is the God of Christianity."

As Stough raced home, Pepper Hamilton's legal assistant Kate Henson called him with the good news. He stopped by his house and sent a brief e-mail to his friends and family. "Judge rules in our favor. Intelligent design not science. No shit."

Later, Stough remembered that his pastor was on his e-mail list.

Sneath dressed and rushed to Christy Rehm's house. When

Sneath arived, Rehm was blasting the Pearl Jam song "Do the Evolution." The two women jumped in Rehm's car and drove north on Route 74 for Harrisburg. They passed one of the ousted board members, James Cashman, standing in his used-car lot. Silly with excitement, they couldn't resist. Sneath leaned out the window, and gave the man the finger. Rehm laid on her horn and yelled, "Loserrrrr!"

At Dover High School, Jess Kitzmiller's French teacher stopped her in the hall with the news. Jess told her friends. Soon, the news had traveled around the school. Science teachers Bertha Spahr and Rob Eshbach, breathless with vindication, hugged each other. Jones had also criticized the disrespect shown to Dover's teachers. "The Board brazenly chose not to follow the advice of their only science-education resources as the teachers were not included in the process of drafting the language adopted by the Board Curriculum Committee," he said.

When Stough walked into the Pepper Hamilton office, a woman at the front desk greeted him with a copy of the full decision. In the lobby, he and others sat on chairs pulled into a circle and tried to go over it from the beginning. But every time Stough started to read, someone yelled out, "Oh my God. Look at page 85!" Or "62!" or "112!"

Within ninety minutes of the announcement, members of the Discovery Institute, their worst fears realized, blasted the ruling from Seattle. In a press release, John West wrote, "The Dover decision is an attempt by an activist federal judge to stop the spread of a scientific idea and even to prevent criticism of Darwinian evolution through government-imposed censorship rather than open debate, and it won't work."

But throughout the trial, Jones learned much about Discovery's tactics and he had anticipated such a response. "Those who disagree with our holding will likely mark it as the product of an activist judge," he wrote. "If so, they will have erred as this is manifestly not an activist Court. Rather, this case came to us as the result of the activism of an ill-informed faction on a school board, aided by a national public interest law firm eager to find a constitutional test case on ID, who in combination drove the Board to adopt an imprudent and ultimately unconstitutional policy."

Jones decreed Discovery's fallback "teach the controversy" strategy a fraud.

"ID's backers have sought to avoid the scientific scrutiny which we have now determined that it cannot withstand by advocating that the controversy, but not ID itself, should be taught in science class. This tactic is at best disingenuous, and at worst a canard. The goal of the IDM is not to encourage critical thought, but to foment a revolution which would supplant evolutionary theory with ID."

At the press conference later that day, reporters and camera crews packed Pepper Hamilton's conference room. The parents and attorneys squeezed by the media, barely able to fit inside.

Callahan sat between Walczak and Rothschild, grinning up at their smiling faces. In the back row, Christy Rehm and Tammy Kitzmiller fidgeted and poked each other. Pastor Eshbach, who warned board members eighteen months earlier that they would divide the community, stood quietly, watching from a corner. Plaintiff Joel Leib wore a huge satisfied smile on his face. In his decision, Jones quoted Leib, who traces his family back to Dover's original settlers. "It's driven a wedge where there hasn't been a wedge before. People are afraid to talk to people for fear, and that's happened to me. They're afraid to talk to me because I'm on the wrong side of the fence."

Jones referenced Justice Brennan's opinion in *Edwards v. Aguil-*

lard that a board's articulation of secular purpose "must be sincere and not a sham."

Jones wrote, "Although Defendants attempt to persuade this Court that each Board member who voted for the biology curriculum change did so for the secular purpose of improving science education and to exercise critical thinking skills, their contentions are simply irreconcilable with the record evidence. Their asserted purposes are a sham."

"Thank you, Judge Jones," Kitzmiller said at the press conference. "Thank you for listening."

Eugenie Scott handed Stough a T-shirt listing the names of hundreds of scientists named Steve who support evolution. NCSE had made Stough an honorary member of "Project Steve Steve," a campaign stressing the validity of evolutionary theory and created in honor of Harvard evolutionary biologist Stephen Jay Gould. NCSE's point is that evolution has overwhelming support since scientists named Steve make up one percent of the scientific community. Stough's name had been included on the T-shirt. He held up the shirt for the cameras and grinned.

After the reporters packed up their cameras and microphones, the plaintiffs and their lawyers, joined by Dover's science teachers, headed off to a bar. As the news traveled around the world, they celebrated. Stough received a call from a reporter in New Zealand. Barrie Callahan's friend, vacationing in Malaysia, saw her on her hotel room's television. In Australia, the daughter of another friend heard Callahan's voice on the radio.

Jones, meanwhile, sat down to a quiet dinner with his wife. He ate with the television on, watching the news.

In a written statement released later that day by his law firm, Thompson said, "The Founders of this country would be astonished at the thought that this simple curriculum change 'established religion' in violation of the Constitution that they drafted."

He said the Supreme Court's interpretation of the Establishment Clause in the past forty years—since the banning of organized prayer and teacher-led Bible readings in public schools—is "in hopeless disarray."

"The district court's decision today continues along this path of applying a fundamentally flawed jurisprudence. Unfortunately, until the Supreme Court adopts a more coherent and historically sound jurisprudence, school districts like Dover will be at risk of costly lawsuits by the ACLU for adopting such modest curriculum changes such as the one at issue."

One has to wonder whether Thompson ever expected to sway the verdict. His prize, he said, always had been the U.S. Supreme Court. Which may be why he seldom appeared to try during the trial. He was just biding his time, fighting a battle for public opinion. He wanted those on the Christian right to believe that an injustice had taken place in Dover.

Barrie Callahan found the irony delicious. Thompson's professed religious revolution had been thwarted by the democratic process. With a newly elected school board in opposition to the now unconstitutional intelligent design policy, any chance of an appeal was dead. Voters didn't want a revolution. They wanted the saga to end. They dismissed Thompson's arguments and cleansed the temple.

As for Behe, he assured me he'd talk to me after the filing of the decision. He gave me the phone number where he could be reached. I called several times. He never answered. I left voicemail messages. He never called back.

My colleague Michelle Starr, with a copy of the decision in her hand, visited Bonsell's radiator repair shop. Until Starr handed him the verdict's final pages, Bonsell hadn't heard the news. Staring down at the words in his hand, Bonsell appeared shocked, Starr remembers. "The inescapable truth is that both Bonsell and Buckingham lied . . ." Jones wrote.

Was it possible that Bonsell hadn't expected Jones to call him a liar? That he thought he could get away with swearing, under oath, that he had no idea where the money came from to buy the *Pandas* textbook, then admit, in court, that he actually knew all along? Darwin wrote in *Descent of Man*, "ignorance more frequently begets confidence than does knowledge."

Jones was under no delusion that no one had ever before lied in his courtroom. But there was a brazenness to what he had witnessed. He couldn't ignore what Buckingham and Bonsell had done, he said. After he grilled Bonsell, Jones gathered copies of school board members' depositions and court transcripts. He sent the information down to the federal courthouse's second floor to the U.S. Attorney's office with the recommendation that it investigate Dover's school board members for perjury.

"The citizens of the Dover area were poorly served by the members of the Board who voted for the ID Policy," Jones wrote in his decision. "It is ironic that several of these individuals, who so staunchly and proudly touted their religious convictions in public, would time and again lie to cover their tracks and disguise the real purpose behind the ID Policy."

When reporters called Buckingham at his home in North Carolina, the fragile man who limped into the courtroom for his testimony had disappeared. Rather, the blustery cop picked up the phone. "If he says I'm a liar, then he's a liar," Buckingham said. "I think Judge Jones ought to be ashamed of himself. I'm still waiting for a judge or anyone to show me anywhere in the Constitution where there's a separation of church and state."

At the conclusion of the Scopes Trial, H.L. Mencken wrote, "Even a superstitious man has certain inalienable rights. He has a right to harbor and indulge his imbecilities as long as he pleases, provided only he does not try to inflict them upon other men by force. He has a right to argue for them as eloquently as he can, in season and out of season. He has a right to teach them to his children. But certainly he has no right to be protected against the free criticism of those who do not hold them. He has no right to demand that they be treated as sacred. He has no right to preach them without challenge."

If Walczak had worshipped my father's Jesus, Dean Lebo would have adored him.

But my father believed, as many fundamentalist Christians do, that the ACLU is a Communist-inspired plot against God. "You mean, the American Communist Lawyers Union?" he'd ask, and chuckle like I never heard that joke before. I'd sigh and roll my eyes.

This is an issue of lasting confusion for me. Why do evangelicals conflate an organization that champions the U.S. Constitution and the rights of individual liberties to a political party that embraces totalitarian government and collective ownership?

"We're the antithesis of communism," Walczak said.

Walczak often pretends to be cynical, and maybe he is, but he also holds dearly such romantic notions as fairness and equality—all the things, actually, that my father and other evangelicals say they believe in.

His family emigrated from Europe. His mother's side of the family were Holocaust victims. His Jewish grandmother died at Treblinka. His grandfather, a lawyer and violinist, escaped the Polish death camp and devoted the rest of his life to testifying about the war crimes he witnessed. Walczak's mother, only eight years old at the start of World War II, was hidden by a Christian family and survived. After the war, she reunited with her father.

Walczak's story sounds like an evangelical testimony. In high school, he didn't know what interested him or where he wanted to take his life. He played soccer in the afternoons and otherwise hung out with friends, doing little studying.

He applied, and was accepted, to Colgate University through its early admissions program. Failing his senior classes, Walczak knew that if he waited to apply, the school would deny him based on his later transcripts. He continued partying through his freshman year of college, disinterested in studying, and landed on academic probation. But, one class, a freshman seminar taught by a former CIA agent, sparked an interest in civil rights. Walczak became interested in social change through nonviolent protest. He studied the teachings of Mahatma Gandhi and Dr. Martin Luther King Jr. He wrestled with ethics, became a philosophy major, and began trying to figure out how to order his life. He met Kathy, a blond cheerleader studying to be a doctor, and the woman he'd eventually marry. Walczak decided his life should have purpose. In 1983, just after he graduated, he traveled to Poland to take part in Lech Walesa's Solidarity Movement. The country was under martial law in order to silence the anti-communist activists. Despite accounts in the international press, the underground movement was growing. Walczak took photos and collected pamphlets. He remembers walking up a street in Gdansk with a shipyard worker. As an American who took free speech for granted, he spoke openly of his outrage at government injustice. The big man put his hand over Walczak's mouth and warned him that such talk was dangerous.

One day, a spontaneous Solidarity demonstration broke out. As the shipyard workers rallied, "the cops came in and started whacking people with nightsticks," Walczak said. He snapped pictures, but officers blindsided him, throwing him to the ground. They tried to seize his Nikon, but he wrapped his body protectively around the camera. A group of shipyard workers, built like line-backers, yanked him from the officers. They yelled for him to run as they blocked the officers with their bodies.

"It was like out of a movie," Walczak says. Chased by the police through the cobblestone streets, he and his friends jumped on a streetcar just as the doors closed.

Realizing that he was now likely targeted by police, he met with the U. S. Consul in a cavernous Soviet-style building. Walczak started to talk about the photos and underground pamphlets, but the man shushed him. He turned up the volume of a transistor radio and motioned for Walczak to whisper in his ear. He told Walczak to leave the material behind. He promised that he would forward it to the United States in a diplomatic pouch.

Walczak left Poland on a train. Border police entered the private car and demanded to see Walczak's papers. The officer ordered him to undress and searched him. Shaken, Walczak realized he would have been arrested had he been found with the photographs and pamphlets. When he returned home, he said, "there was no doubt in my mind I wanted to be a civil-liberties attorney," he said.

His cluttered office is on the second floor of a narrow building in a funky section of Pittsburgh dotted with ethnic storefront restaurants. At the building's kitchen sink, a sign instructs staff and visitors alike to wash their own coffee cups. Private law firms may have offered him better paying jobs, but he's never looked back. And while Walczak isn't much of a believer in God, he said he credited his path in life to fate. But where Walczak and evangelicals differ is that he strives for justice here on Earth, not salvation and retribution in the next life.

If he could wave a magic wand to be a believer, would he? Walczak doesn't know. He's always had a hard time reconciling the fact that bad things happen to good people. He has trouble ignoring the harmful things being done in the Lord's name. The God fundamentalists believe in, "a smiter for infinite transgressions," is not a God he wants to believe in.

An e-mail from him three days before Judge Jones's verdict prompted my last fight with my father. Walczak wrote of the Christmas cookies with three kinds of sprinkles that he had been baking that evening with his family. He mentioned the hand-carved manger in his living room.

His e-mail had been in response to a facetious reference I made about the ACLU's "War on Christmas." Fox News' Bill O'Reilly, joined by a cadre of outspoken fundamentalists, had mounted a media campaign to decry a liberal "conspiracy" to obscure the religious aspect of the holiday. But O'Reilly's conspiracy had no basis in reality.[1] Still, that didn't keep the evangelicals from parroting the talking points. That night, my father brought up the War on Christmas, of the "politically correct" movement to force Christ out of Christmas.

I berated him for his willingness to buy into such a lie. I said something, which I'm sure made little sense, about hand-carved mangers and, "Three kinds of sprinkles, Dad!" He looked at me, startled, and left the room. The next morning, he awakened thinking of me. "Why is she so angry?" he asked my mother.

My father was a frugal man who, when he bought a cup of take-out coffee, took great pleasure in reusing the cardboard cup until it disintegrated in his hands. "I've been using that one for about a month," he'd say, turning the cup to show off its sad decay. He measured the world in $12 increments—the price to feed a child in Haiti for a month. To him, every $12 saved meant one less hungry child. He'd ask how much I'd spent on my hair, then do the calculations. "That'd feed eight children," he'd say, nodding his head.

For years, my father had a beat-up pair of red sneakers. Stained with frayed laces, he refused to replace them. Finally, when they were falling apart at the soles, flip-flopping when he walked, he splurged and bought himself a new pair. The idea of him buying something not only brand new, but from a real store, and not the Salvation Army, was a strange one. In our family, this was news. The story spread quickly.

One day in December a teenage boy with a girlfriend and a baby came into the radio station. My father sent him to the up-stairs apartment to comb through the used clothing he collected for others. He told the young father to take whatever he found. The boy saw the new sneakers, exactly his size and still nestled in their box. He came downstairs with them on his feet. My father smiled. It wasn't until later that the boy learned he had taken my father's shoes.

Nine days after Judge Jones's decision, my father laced up the beat-up sneakers with the worn-out soles and drove to one of the local prisons, just as he did every Thursday. A member of Second-Chance Ministries, he'd sit and witness with prisoners, talking to them about salvation. In my father's world, all things had purpose and nothing could be so worn and useless that it should be tossed away. He practiced this whether it was with a coffee cup or a man's life.

He continued to help the men, those who wanted his help, after they were released. He found them jobs and cars and apart-ments. For months, one man, Larry Ray, slept on the floor of the radio station until he was strong enough to live on his own. Ray became my father's closest friend. Two weeks earlier, my father confided to him that he had suffered a heart attack while sitting in church. My father believed in faith healing. He chose God over science. He swore Ray to secrecy and never visited a doctor.

On this particular Thursday at the Cumberland County jail,

my father saw a man milling about with the other prisoners. He had never met him before. But, as he said the Lord so often did for him, he told the prisoner that he felt led to speak with him. In the middle of prayer, my father rested his head on the table, his Bible next to him. The prisoner waited a bit, thinking maybe my father had fallen asleep. Doctors said he died of a massive coronary.

12

The Sheep and the Goats

I'm ready to go, when he comes my way, he could come tomorrow.
He could come today.

—*If Jesus Came Today, sung by Bill Jones*
and the Bluegrass Travelers

It's been a strange year.

I woke up on New Year's Day, realizing that I, along with the rest of my agnostic family, had inherited a fundamentalist Christian radio station.

Several weeks into the year, I ran into Pastor Grove as he was picketing evolution outside a York theater. Nearby, a man dressed as an ape jumped around and danced. Grove clutched a Bible, as his supporters waved signs that read, "Evolution is a lie." I was covering a play based on the Scopes case, *The Great Tennessee Monkey Trial*. Reluctantly, but because it's my job, I approached Grove for the requisite comment. Yet again, he told me that one can't believe in God unless you accept the Bible as literal truth. "You might as well just throw it away," he said, pretending to drop his King James Version into a trash can.

Grove knew my father. He told me he was sorry to hear about his death. "He was a good Christian," Grove said. And then, "You know, you can be with him again." All it would take, he explained, thrusting his Bible in my face, was for me to renounce evolution and beg for forgiveness.

He gave me a meaningful look and patted me on the arm. I nodded, unable to speak.

In February, plaintiffs' attorneys settled their costs with the school district. As part of the verdict, the plaintiffs' attorneys were entitled to recoup their legal fees. The original price tag was about $2.5 million, but they only asked for $1 million. The Pepper Hamilton law firm, which incurred most of the expenses, donated all but a tiny portion of its money to the ACLU and the Americans United for Separation of Church and State. The awkwardness of handing a bill to the newly elected school board that had opposed the intelligent design policy was not lost on the lawyers. But as Rothschild said in news accounts at the time, they also believed they needed to make the message clear: "The threat of a lawsuit is real when the Constitution is violated. It's important to recognize here, with this case, the substantial expense to bring and win this lawsuit."

The rift in Dover remains, but most of the time, people get along. At the tiny Italian restaurant just outside the borough, those who had fought on different sides sit at tables only a few feet apart. While they're not exactly friendly, they exchange curt nods and everyone eats in peace.

In June 2006, two years after Buckingham and Bonsell first spoke publicly about creationism, the new school board members took their seats in the elementary school cafeteria for their regular monthly meeting. On the agenda, the officials had scheduled a vote on whether to search for a new district superintendent. Richard Nilsen, his contract about to expire, could still apply for his job if he wanted to. Board members had assured him they couldn't guarantee anything.

As superintendent, Nilsen had helped guide Dover into what Judge Jones referred to as a "legal maelstrom." At the very least, he showed contempt for the process and obfuscated the truth.

Once the new board took office, Nilsen knew his days were numbered, and he dusted off his resume. Alan Bonsell and other former school board members were outraged. Why would the new school board do this to their superintendent?

In the brightly lit room painted with murals of dancing vegetables and cartons of milk, they stepped up to the podium for public comment, taking turns addressing officials. Bonsell, under investigation for perjury, accused the new board of being vindictive. He said former board members supported Nilsen. He warned them to be careful, because he and others would remember what they did and oust them from office in the next election.

"To get rid of Dr. Nilsen is to get rid of the best superintendent in York County, in my opinion," Bonsell said. Sheila Harkins brought her dictionary to the podium and read the definition of the word "discussion."

"To debate, argue in detail," she said. Eighteen months earlier, Harkins gaveled down any attempts to publicly discuss intelligent design. Now, she scolded board members because they wouldn't debate Nilsen's contract in front of residents.

Alan's father, Donald Bonsell, stood up and said the board's actions were "disgraceful."

The elder Bonsell, who had led the scheme to keep hidden the source of money to purchase *Pandas*, alleged a conspiracy. "There has to be something at work here," Bonsell said, shaking in anger. "I behoove you to be decent and good and love this community. Set aside your biases. You will destroy this community," he warned.

Earlier that day, Bryan and Christy Rehm had driven back from vacation in the Great Smoky Mountains. Their four children stayed behind with Bryan's parents, and the couple planned to return first thing the next morning. As a member of the school board, Bryan needed to be present for the vote. Christy came along on the nine-hour trip because she knew what was going to happen at the meeting. She had something to say about it.

She followed Donald Bonsell to the podium. "After hearing these tales of the Apocalypse, let me remind you, ladies and gentlemen, that you were elected," she said. "They do not represent the voices of this community."

She said that the people who spoke at the meeting still hadn't grasped the damage they had inflicted on their town. Even though voters rejected them, they spoke like people who still expected to get their own way. "Now, they are the saviors," Rehm said.

At the end of the debate, the board voted 5–4 to advertise for a new superintendent.

The national organizations that once championed a revolution have spent the past year busily backpedaling, trying to convince supporters that Jones's decision is irrelevant. As they correctly have pointed out, the verdict doesn't have precedent beyond Dover. But its impact, nonetheless, has been far-reaching. States and school districts across the country watched and paid heed. In Ohio, the state's Board of Education struck down ID-friendly lesson plans. Later, Kansas voters, in the wake of their own contentious battles, ousted anti-evolution members from their Department of Education. On the anniversary of Jones's decision—a day greeted with wishes of "Merry Kitzmas" by plaintiffs and their attorneys—the school district of Cobb County, Georgia, reached a settlement in its lengthy court battle. Following Dover's victory, Rothschild and Americans United's Richard Katskee signed on to the Cobb County case. Katskee, as lead attorney, convinced the Georgia school district to remove warning stickers from biology textbooks that alerted students that evolution "was a theory, not a fact."

But anti-evolution factions continue the fight. The Foundation for Thought and Ethics is releasing its *Pandas* sequel, *The Design of Life*.

A draft of the textbook had been previewed during Dover's trial. Just as FTE substituted the word "creationism" with "intelligent design" throughout versions of *Pandas*, this edition substituted "sudden emergence" for "intelligent design."

Which prompted Rothschild to ask Michael Behe during cross-examination, "Will we be back in a couple of years for the 'sudden emergence' trial?"

To which Judge Jones responded "Not on my docket."

In a newsletter, FTE president Jon Buell assured supporters that the book will present only "the latest scientific data and strongest arguments." Ignoring the pounding the book took in the courtroom, Buell also said it will "accelerate the growing popularity of intelligent design and move our culture to far greater acceptance."

But even as they publish textbooks, intelligent design proponents say, at least in public, that educators are not actually supposed to teach it. The Discovery Institute's Stephen Meyer told a crowd in Knoxville that it is "premature" to teach intelligent design in public schools. Meyer said, "We encourage people not to push this in schools right now."[1]

Even Phillip Johnson, the Berkeley-based godfather of the movement, said intelligent design isn't yet ready for prime time. In an interview after the trial, he said, "I also don't think that there is really a theory of intelligent design at the present time to propose as a comparable alternative to the Darwinian theory, which is, whatever errors it might contain, a fully worked out scheme."[2]

So, after exploiting the religious convictions of fearful evangelicals, after hindering science education and dividing communities across the country, Johnson admitted what had become painfully obvious—intelligent design is a sham.

Still, in this story, one nagging issue remains. What prompted Buckingham, Bonsell, and others to lie? Whose idea was it?

Richard Thompson decries moral relativism, a theme he returned to often outside the courthouse. He blames Darwin for leading us away from absolute truth. Yet he defended people who clearly lied about their actions and slandered others. How was he able to reconcile his moralistic outlook with his clients' disregard for the obvious truth? He must—I can't imagine any other rationale—believe that he was fighting for a purpose greater than the Ninth Commandment: "Thou shalt not bear false witness."

Since the trial, Thompson has not returned several months of phone calls and e-mails requesting an interview, so I don't have an answer to my question.

As the first anniversary of the trial neared, Buckingham called to tell me he was having surgery. He said he just wanted me to know. He sounded a little sad. We chatted for a few minutes about his grandchildren. I wished him well and promised I'd come visit him in the hospital.

A week earlier, I had followed the plaintiffs down to Washington, D.C., to watch them speak at an ACLU conference. They shared a stage alongside the Reverend James Lawson, a civil rights icon—a man, who, when faced with segregation and bigotry, organized nonviolent protests and lunch-counter sit-ins. He brought people together and taught them to stand up to unjust laws because he believed the Bill of Rights belongs to his people, too.

I wanted to introduce myself to the Reverend Lawson and tell him how much I admired him, but I was strangely overcome with shyness. Steve Stough approached Lawson for me. I gushed and shook his hand, which was large and strong but had the papery feel of skin worn smooth by time. I choked back a few tears and told him it was an honor to meet him.

People possessing similar stories of courage filled the large conference hotel. Still, the Dover parents stood out. They couldn't cross a room without someone stopping them to shake their hands and to thank them for standing up to religious bullying. When a woman approached Stough, gushing over him as I had Lawson, I fell back and got out of the way. From a distance, I watched, and I could feel the grin on my face. As a reporter, I guess I'm not supposed to feel this way. Yet, I thought of how pleased and proud I am to know these people.

They spoke before a filled ballroom. The Rehms, the Callahans, Sneath, Fenimore, Stough, Eveland, and Walczak. Bryan Rehm recalled a friend's suggestion that if he didn't like what was happening in Dover, he should move somewhere else.

"But if I don't do something here, where's it going to spread next?" he said to the audience.

Rothschild had spoken of the parents' love for their children that "spilled out of that witness stand and filled this courtroom." He was right. But they also exuded love for this country. A love of truth. A love for the idea that a few people standing together can still make a difference.

While still wrestling with these notions, I sat down with Judge Jones in his spacious chambers overlooking the patina of the Harrisburg Capitol's copper dome. I had come to interview him about the case, and as I looked out the window, I noticed that the leaves' colors had changed from green to orange and red.

Jones suffered from allergies, and his eyes were puffy. Margaret Talbot, writing in *The New Yorker* about the trial, described Jones as "a rugged 1940s movie star, a cross between William Holden and Robert Mitchum." On this day, he possessed no smoky Robert Mitchum stare. He said he was exhausted from juggling a full docket and speaking engagements around the country. He apologized and said he had to leave early to talk to a local Boy Scout troop that night. "They asked," he said, a little weary.

Just as it had been for many of us, the year following the decision had been something of an emotional roller coaster for him.

Wired magazine named him one of its top 10 "Sexiest Geeks." *Time* magazine picked him as one of 2005's 100 Most Influential People. At the awards dinner, actor Will Smith saw him and shook his hand, thanking him for the decision. A Philadelphia son, Smith said, "You make me proud to be from Pennsylvania." Stephen Colbert walked by and pointed his finger at him. "Judge Jones," he said. Jones pointed his finger back and said, "Stephen Colbert." As Colbert passed by, he said quietly, "Intelligent design, seemed like a pretty good idea at the time, didn't it?"

"Yes, I guess it did," Jones said, tickled.

But accolades weren't all he received. Jones received hateful e-mail messages so strident that following his decision, U. S. Marshals watched over his home and family over Christmas.

He wasn't the only one to get threatening mail. Soon after the verdict, Kitzmiller's daughter tossed an envelope on the kitchen table. It was unsigned and came with no return address.

"Madalyn Murray O'Hair was murdered . . .," it said, referring to the woman whose 1960 lawsuit led to the banning of organized prayer and teacher-led Bible readings in public schools. O'Hair disappeared in 1995, along with her adopted daughter. In 2001, her killer led investigators to the shallow Texas grave where the woman's mutilated body had been buried.

The letter writer knew of Kitzmiller's daughters. The person wrote of the bad things that can happen to the children of sinners. "I sure would hate to be in your shoes, or your daughters shoes. God hates sin. All these young people being killed in auto wrecks look out when your day comes. . . . Watch out for a bullet."

Conservative pundits accused Jones of betrayal and threw connip-tions. Phyllis Schlafly said Jones owed his position "entirely to the evangelical Christians who pulled the lever for George W. Bush in 2002." She said he had "stuck the knife in the backs of those who brought him to the dance."[3]

Fox News's Bill O'Reilly called him "a fascist," and Ann Coulter said, "The Darwinists have saved the secular sanctity of their temples: the public schools. They didn't win on science, persuasion, or the evidence. They won the way liberals always win: by finding a court to hand them everything they want on a silver platter."

Noting that Coulter "foments a kind of civic stupidity, in my opinion,"[4] Jones spent much of the year addressing the issue of ju-dicial independence, pointing out to audiences that she and others woefully misinterpret a judge's responsibility. He told me he has tried to use his post-Kitzmiller glory as a window of opportunity, turning his speeches into mini–civics lessons. In a speech he gave to the Anti-Defamation League,[5] Jones said accusations that he is "an activist judge" point to a problem that "threatens to, I think, tear at the fabric of our system of justice in the United States.

"The premise of Ms. Schlafly and some others seems to be that judges can and should act in a partisan manner rather than strictly adhering to the rule of law. Now, to those who believe that judges must cast aside precedents and rule as according to an agenda, let me say that I believe that the public's dependence upon the im-partiality and the integrity of judges is absolutely essential to its confidence in our system of justice."

Sitting in his chambers, he said that his critics eyed his Re-publican pedigree and assumed he would be an activist judge on their behalf. They figured he could be counted on to help tear down the wall of separation between church and state. But if the courtroom door had swung open during the trial, and Thomas Jefferson himself had appeared and witnessed the defense's attempt to force its religious views on others, Jones told me he is confident the founding father would have said, "No, this is not acceptable."

That day, he and I talked for hours about this bright shiny moment that was *Kitzmiller v. Dover*, and how we've all been changed by this experience. This, we agreed, was a time when the system really worked.

Jones walked me to the door of his chambers. He was running late for the Boy Scouts meeting, but I could tell he regretted ending the interview. We lingered in the doorway. I told him that, yes, Dover was proof the system worked, but what about the next time? In the past couple of years there have been many attacks on this country's civil liberties. Jones smiled and reassured me. It will work out, he said, because he has faith in this nation. "Democracy is messy," he said, shaking my hand. "It's supposed to be that way."

Rob Eshbach sat with students in quiet classrooms after school, speaking of balancing science with his faith. Jen Miller inspired students to gaze down long hallways and into our past. But these children of pastors always taught evolution with trepidation, afraid of offending creationist beliefs. This year, that's changed. Miller has revamped the biology curriculum. The teaching of evolutionary theory will no longer be crammed into a handful of days out of the school year. Now, teachers start with evolution—because everything in biology builds from the theory.

Bryan Rehm says Dover high school is now the safest place in the country to teach science. Attacks on evolution continue in other classrooms, in other places, quietly, out of sight of newspaper reporters and public scrutiny. But not in Dover. Too many people are now watching.

Both he and his wife teach in a rural school district just over the York County line. In meetings, Rehm listens to science teachers in his department espouse creationist beliefs. They question the fact of evolutionary theory. Christy endures the pointed questions from a clique of girls—they call themselves, "the God Girls"—who want to know why they should have to learn anything in science class that isn't based on the Bible.

Knowing she was a Dover plaintiff, the girls ask her if she's an atheist, and Christy assures them she's not. But they don't believe her. Not really.

The Rehms find it frustrating that the students who challenge them understand so little about the points they're espousing. They talk about gaps in the fossil record. They say DNA evidence refutes common descent. But they are only parroting the uninformed remarks of others. All these students know is that in their hearts, there is no room for both science and faith. To the Rehms, it all feels so familiar.

One sunny winter day after the verdict, I visited Alan Bonsell in his radiator repair shop. He told me he wasn't sure if he wanted to talk to me. And then, standing next to a car with an open hood, we talked for more than an hour and a half. Bonsell remains bitter about the lack of a court appeal. "The Supreme Court would have ruled in our favor," he said.

Which may be why Bonsell was able to sit through the entire trial with that smile on his face. Why he was able to turn to a federal judge and lie to him. He wasn't concerned with what played out within the courtroom. He was more concerned with what would happen later.

Because, with Bonsell and Buckingham and all fundamentalist

Christians, everything about now is irrelevant. It's always about later.

"Ken Ham didn't convince you?" he asked when I told him I subscribe to the creationist's magazine. When I told him no, he accused me of not doing my research. He said I must read the Bible. I told him that I've been working my way through it. This is still not good enough. I have to study it, he said, stressing the word "study." The Old Testament has 250 prophecies of the coming of Christ, he said. That's statistically impossible to be a coincidence. That was the second time in our conversation he used the phrase "statistically impossible."

Earlier, he cited the oft-repeated creationist claim that genetic mutations are ninety-five percent of the time bad or harmful, making evolution "statistically impossible." But what Bonsell doesn't understand is that harmful mutations typically don't survive long in a population. Just as Jen Miller tries to show her students, natural selection over millions of years is what makes change through genetic mutations possible. But because Bonsell believes the earth is only six thousand years old, this, of course, doesn't work.

I'd heard everything Bonsell said. I can cite sources for almost all his information. But as we talked, I realized that he can't. At one point, he suggested that the bone of a Tyrannosaurus rex still containing soft tissue was found recently in Montana, proving that the fossil couldn't be millions of years old.

I'm familiar with this story. I said the soft tissue was actually a small number of cells encapsulated in a mineral tomb. The find was significant, but it didn't discount the fossil record. But Bonsell didn't listen. I heard the arrogance behind his remarks. I will have never done enough homework to have an informed opinion. Because no opinion matters other than accepting Christ as your savior.

Our conversation dissolved into an argument.

He told me with contempt that Ken Miller, the plaintiffs' lead scientific witness, testified during the trial that a theory is as good as a fact.

"I mean, I couldn't believe he said that," Bonsell said.

This was the moment I realized that I was the fool here. Bonsell, as president of his local school board, led Dover into a national test case of a religious scheme he still argues is a scientific theory. He sat in the same courtroom as I did for six weeks, listening to amazing testimony laying out an overwhelming body of evidence that proved that evolution is a fact.

Even the statement read to students, which he claims to have helped draft, provides a clear and succinct definition of a scientific theory—the only sentence out of the four paragraphs that was not misleading: "A theory is defined as a well-tested explanation that unifies a broad range of observations."

And yet, even after the trial, Bonsell had not grasped the difference between a scientific theory and a hunch.

Standing in front of me with his arms crossed, he looked at me and accused me of not thinking critically, because surely if I did, I would know that Christ was born of a virgin and that the entire fossil record was created by a single flood.

Where the hell did I get the idea I was going to get any insight here?

I asked him why he didn't do his homework, why he and the rest of the board were so ill-informed about intelligent design? Why do I know more about his creationist arguments than he does?

He said the statement read to students was only four paragraphs and it wasn't a big deal. I told him, no, he's wrong. He knew he was leading Dover into a lawsuit. Lawyers had even written a letter before filing the suit, urging board members to drop the policy. Yet Bonsell persisted in his attorney's religious revolution. So why didn't he do his homework?

He told me he didn't need to read *Pandas* because it wasn't in the classroom. This is untrue. The school board moved the textbooks to the library only after parents filed their lawsuit.

He said the difference between us is that if he's wrong, he's not hurt. If I'm wrong . . . well, I'm going to hell.

I changed the subject. I asked about his wife and her cancer. When he talked about Brenda, his eyes softened. He told me she's gone five years with a clean bill of health and is now in remission. He told me it's terrible watching his wife, his partner, his best friend, go through something like that and be unable to fix the problem.

I told him I can imagine.

Bonsell looked at me a little bit more closely, as if he might have never really looked at me before. He told me he can't imagine going through that without faith. He said it would be terrible for me to have to endure the death of a loved one without belief that another life awaits us.

And I replied, "You're right."

For months after his death, I remained angry that my father and I had not resolved our argument, that I was unable, ultimately, to make him understand that these people mocked his faith with their lies. I tried to carry on a one-sided debate without him. I spent a lot of time with fundamentalists at the radio station and through my job at the newspaper. I couldn't walk past a street preacher without stopping to talk, opening up my heart.

But they, and I've learned this is often true, don't really care about my heart. They're only interested in my soul.

I spent a lot of time imagining the conversation—if only I

could—that I would have with my father. For months I rehashed stories of the trial in my head, thinking that maybe this would have convinced him. That he would say, yes, this isn't what Christianity is supposed to be about.

But time passed and as the days began to grow cooler, I mellowed a bit. I had been meaning to get seed to fill my birdfeeders. On snowy mornings, I used to call my father and tell him about the birds outside my window.

My father frequently cooked whole turkeys and then, because he could never waste anything, would throw the bones and skin and gizzard and neck onto the roof of the post office next to the radio station.

Between sips of coffee, I'd tell him, "There are six chickadees and four goldfinches at the feeder."

He'd look out the second-floor window of the radio station. "There are three crows working on that turkey carcass," he'd tell me. "The one's got a big piece. I don't know if he's gonna be able to take off with it. He's trying."

If I could have one more conversation, I'd forget all about intelligent design. I wouldn't be interested in discussing evolution and revolution and salvation.

I'd just like to ask him if the crows have carried off that turkey carcass yet.

On the way to visit Buckingham in the hospital, I stopped at a store to pick up a get-well card. Sitting in my car, I struggled over what to write on the inside. Finally, I settled on, "I'm praying for you. Lauri."

So I wouldn't be lying, before I licked the envelope, I ran through my head, "Please God, help Bill with his health problems."

I walked into the hospital, and from down the hall, I saw Buckingham in a hospital gown, struggling to walk, a nurse holding on to his arm. I saw a tired old man in pain. I had to turn away.

Later, I sat in a chair at the foot of his hospital bed as a registered nurse showed a student how to set up Buckingham's antibiotic IV. His knee, which poked out from under the sheets, was wrapped in white gauze. Sunshine streamed through the window and onto his bed. He held his left arm still as the nurse adjusted the lines that held the fluid flowing into his body.

The older woman explained that the primary bag, filled with the antibiotics, had to be higher than the secondary saline bag.

"I guess you know all about this, don't cha Bill?" I asked him.

"I've heard it before, but I don't know it," he said.

I smiled, but I thought, "No. I guess you don't."

I am one of his few visitors, he told me. The people from his church have not come to see him. Once they willingly opened their pocketbooks to help him finance his religious mission to buy the *Pandas* textbook. But he had a disagreement with a new pastor. He stopped going to the church. And the people there didn't come to visit him.

Neither did any of the former board members. Not Bonsell, not Harkins, not Rowand. After Buckingham told me he was having surgery, I e-mailed Rowand to let him know. He didn't respond.

Buckingham grasped my hand tightly and held on. He looked at me intently and told me he trusts me. He told me he considers me to be his friend. Me. A religiously ambivalent member of the liberal media who had told him to his face that I believed he lied.

I am his friend? Because these people who professed to be Christians then bore false witness? Nothing holds them together.

For they are like the foolish man, who built his house on the sand.

One of my father's favorite scriptures was Matthew 25:31–46, in which the Lord sent the sheep to heaven because of their good deeds. As for the goats, Christ told them, "I was a stranger, and ye took me not in: naked, and ye clothed me not: sick, and in prison, and ye visited me not.

"Then shall they also answer him, saying, Lord, when saw we thee an hungered, or athirst, or a stranger, or naked, or sick, or in prison, and did not minister unto thee? Then shall he answer them, saying, Verily I say unto you, Inasmuch as ye did it not to one of the least of these, ye did it not to me."

I remain part of this community. And part of me is reluctant to write quite so frankly about Buckingham and Bonsell and Harkins and the rest. But I remind myself that I have been honest with them. I've told them I believe in evolutionary theory. I've told Buckingham and Harkins that I think they were dishonest. I can't turn away from the truth. They have found no humility. To this day, Buckingham calls Judge Jones's decision a case of "unjustifiable homicide."

But Buckingham, despite his untruths, can be confoundingly endearing. We have had long discussions about bluegrass music. I listen as he tells me tales of Ralph Stanley, Bill Monroe, and local firehouse jams.

I can say this: Buckingham is one heck of a storyteller. And it can never be said that I don't love a good story.

Today, the parents who sued the school district are friends. They remain close with the attorneys, scientists, and teachers. And somehow, strangely, I've become part of that, too. Once the trial was over and I was no longer writing newspaper articles about the case, the admiration I held for these people drifted into friendship.

Kitzmiller and I struck a deal. She is going to dig up her extra strawberry plants in exchange for a few of my heirloom tomato seedlings. My husband listens to Cyndi Sneath and me chattering away and laughing. He shakes his head and says, "You're like two fucking peas in a pod."

Steve Stough and I sit in the Racehorse drinking beer and talking about this idea that we are outsiders. He says he used to feel that way, but he doesn't anymore.

The parents didn't know each other, but they were brought together because they all believed that you don't just profess your faith. Because they believed, as my father did, you have to put your beliefs into practice.

And, I wonder, in this story, who are the sheep and who are the goats?

On March 9, 2007, Maxwell Dean Young arrived promptly as scheduled, born a few blocks from the federal courthouse at Harrisburg Hospital.

He is fair, like his mother—my youngest sister, Lesli—and has the same upturned nose as his father, Charlie.

He is the first of Dean Lebo's grandchildren who will not know him.

He is also the first one whom my father will not baptize. I have no proof, only faith, that my father—who found God's guiding hand in each new life—baptized his grandchildren and his great-granddaughter. Not in a church, and with no formal baptismal of record. But in a quiet moment, alone at the kitchen sink, when no one was looking, each baby held in the crook of my father's arm. A few dribbled drops from the tap and a few whispered words in a tiny ear. If I can be sure of anything, I am sure of this.

My mother watches Max for signs that perhaps my father, somewhere, whispers in his ear and makes him smile. She tells me this and I look away, ashamed of myself because I can't reassure her. I'm afraid I will steal her faith with a careless word.

I will teach Max, along with my nieces and other nephews, my grandchildren, those here now and those who will certainly follow, to dream of possibility. This is all I can offer. I will stretch out on the grass with them on hot August nights and together we will shine a flashlight at the stars and ponder infinity until we grow dizzy.

Acknowledgments

I marvel at the generosity of spirit that has been shown me by so many people. The support I have received from everyone has been truly humbling. First of all, I must thank Dover's science teachers and plaintiffs, especially Steve Stough, Bryan and Christy Rehm, and Barrie Callahan—but most of all Cyndi Sneath. They have all shared with me moments of beauty and inspiration. I hope I have done them justice in my recounting.

I'd also like to thank the plaintiffs' attorneys for their willingness to take the time to help me understand the issues of the case, as well as their openness and candor in relating what this case meant to them. Thank you Steve Harvey, Richard Katskee, Vic Walczak, and especially Eric Rothschild, whose enthusiasm never waned no matter how many times I forced him to recount, just one more time, a key event, legal nuance, or personal reflection. His knowledge and fact-checking expertise also saved me from more than a few embarrassing mistakes. I am indebted.

Greg Bowers, an assistant professor at the Missouri School of Journalism, hates the phrase, "writing coach." But I can think of no better description of him in this instance. In the past year, he has talked me down from more than a couple of ledges, and he has given me some great ideas when I was truly stuck. He has spent years doing his best to teach me to write. I sincerely hope I haven't let him down. I'd also like to thank John Wallingford ("a verb please"), a terrific copy editor at the *Tacoma News Tribune* and a ruthless scourge of the passive voice.

I am grateful to Bill Buckingham, a wonderful storyteller and aficionado of great bluegrass music, for our countless conversations. I hope he still considers me to be his friend.

In addition, I must thank my family, especially my brother Todd, who shouldered the family's burdens and asked for nothing in return. I also thank my husband, Jefferson Pepper, whose eternal patience has been sorely tested, and whose songwriting talent and creativity will always remain my greatest source of inspiration.

I must thank the many scientists who patiently answered all my uninformed questions, especially Nick Matzke and Kevin Padian. Their advice and guidance were invaluable. I'm thankful for the long philosophical conversations over coffee with Burt Humburg, who helped me understand that there can be a place in this world for both science and faith.

I am terribly grateful to The New Press and my wonderful editor, Ellen Adler, who took a chance on an inexperienced writer. I also thank Sheila Kinney, who looked out for me, even though she didn't have to.

Additionally, I'd like to thank all the good folks at the science blog Panda's Thumb (Please do not feed the trolls); the Racehorse Tavern; the *York Dispatch* (the "scrappy" newspaper); and all my friends at the *York Daily Record*. Finally, I thank the Flying Spaghetti Monster, without whose spiritual guidance this book would not have been possible.

Notes

Chapter 2: Neighbor Against Neighbor

1. Larry Hicks, "There Are Already Plenty of Chances to Pray in School," *York Dispatch,* March 1, 2002.
2. Cornelia Dean, "Evolution Takes a Back Seat in U.S. Classes," *New York Times,* February 1, 2005.

Chapter 3: Met on the Battlefield

1. "Events of 2004," National Center for Science Education, www.ncseweb.org/pressroom.asp (accessed November 19, 2007).
2. Ibid.
3. Edward J. Larson, *Summer for the Gods: The Scopes Trial and America's Continuing Debate over Science and Religion* (New York: Basic Books, 1997).
4. Barbara Forrest and Paul R. Gross, *Creationism's Trojan Horse: The Wedge of Intelligent Design* (Oxford University Press, 2004), 17.
5. Phillip Johnson, "How the Evolution Debate Can be Won," Coral Ridge Ministries, www.coralridge.org/specialdocs/evolutiondebate.asp (accessed November 19, 2007).
6. *Creationism's Trojan Horse,* 22.

Chapter 4: Myth of Separation

1. Max Blumenthal, "In Contempt of Courts," *The Nation,* April 11, 2005. "In 1989 Barton published a book titled *The Myth of Separation,* which proclaims, 'This book proves that the separation of church and

state is a myth.' The Baptist Joint Committee on Public Affairs, in a critique of his 1995 documentary *America's Godly Heritage*, stated that it was 'laced with exaggerations, half-truths, and misstatements of fact.'"

2. Evan Ratliff, "The Crusade Against Evolution," *Wired*, October 2004.

3. Interview with Steve Nickol, Republican state representative from Hanover, Pennsylvania, February, 2007.

Chapter 6: Kidnapped by Baptists

1. Peter Baker and Peter Slevin, "Bush Remarks On 'Intelligent Design' Theory Fuel Debate," *Washington Post*, August 3, 2005.

2. According to a Gallup Poll taken in the fall of 2004, forty-five percent of Americans believe "God created human beings pretty much in their present form at one time within the last 10,000 years." Only about a third of respondents believe evolution is "well-supported by evidence." National Center for Science Education, www.ncseweb .org/resources/rncse_content/vol24/7937_the_latest_polls_on_ creationis_12_30_1899.asp (accessed December 30, 2007).

3. Bill Kovach and Tom Rosenstiel, *The Elements of Journalism* (New York: Three Rivers Press, 2001).

4. Ibid, 77.

5. *Creationism's Trojan Horse*, 85.

6. Larry Hicks, "Schaad Not Only 'Officer Down,'" *York Dispatch,* December 8, 2002.

7. "History of Dover," The Greater Dover Historical Society, www .gdhspa.org/HistoryOfDover.htm.

Chapter 10: Seeking Comfort

1. Christina Kauffman, "Robertson: Don't Turn to God," *York Dispatch*, November 16, 2005.

2. American Museum of Natural History, www.amnh.org/exhibitions/ darwin/young/lifelong.php (accessed December 30, 2007).

3. Ibid, www.amnh.org/exhibitions/darwin/idea/wife.php (accessed December 30, 2007).

Chapter 11: "Breathtaking Inanity"

1. A.D., "O'Reilly: 'War' on Christmas part of 'secular progressive agenda,'" *Media Matters for America*, November 21, 2005.

Chapter 12: The Sheep and the Goats

1. Rikki Hall, "Kingdom of Love: Creationists Drop Religion for Intelligence," *Metro Pulse*, April 3, 2007.
2. Michelangelo D'Agostino, "In the matter of Berkeley v. Berkeley," *2006 Berkeley Science Review*.
3. Phyllis Schlafly, "Judge's Unintelligent Rant Against Design." Eagle Forum, January 2006, www.eagleforum.org/column/2006/jan06/06-01-04.html.
4. Judge John E. Jones interviewed on WITF's *Smart Talk*, reported in *York Daily Record/Sunday News*, June 23, 2006.
5. Judge John E. Jones, February 10, 2006, speech to Anti-Defamation League's National Committee Meeting in Palm Beach, Florida.

Index

Adams, John, 61
American Civil Liberties Union (ACLU). *See also* specific attorneys
  conferences of, 211–212
  creationism controversy in Ohio and, 34–35
  Kitzmiller trial and, 71, 207
  legal directors of, 54
  Scopes Monkey Trial and, 38–39
Americans United for Separation of Church and State
  "intelligent design" and, 140–141
  Kitzmiller damages and, 207
  legal director, 55–56
  litigation of test case and, 34, 50, 71
Angie, Sister, 146–147
Answers in Genesis Museum, 40
Anti-Defamation League, 54
Argento, Mike, 115–116, 124, 132, 152, 156
Arkansas, 39–40
Assembly of God, 93

Bacteria flagellum, 116–117, 149–151
Baksa, Mike, 16, 19, 22, 33–34, 60
Baltimore Evening Sun, 39
Barton, David, 60–61
Baugh, Carl, 181–182
Behe, Michael, 43, 116–117, 149–158, 198, 210
Benn, Niles, 123
Benton, Chuck, 91–92
Bernhard-Bubb, Heidi, 23, 76, 83, 121–124, 159–161
Bible
  Dover school board meetings and, 24
  laws prohibiting teaching contradictory to, 39
  literal belief in, 3
  lying and, 129
  quotes from, 8, 69, 138, 149, 222
Big Bang theory, 136, 155
Bill Jones and Bluegrass Travelers, 206
biology curriculum. *See also* creationism; intelligent design; *Of Pandas and People*
  Dover school board debate over, 21–25, 29, 33, 45
  "Intelligent design statement" and, 62, 80–81, 84–86, 122, 134
Biology (Prentice-Hall), 24, 29, 33, 114

bird evolution, 133
Blind Watchmaker (Dawkins), 42
Bonsell, Alan
  anonymous donation of *Of Pandas and People* to Dover schools, 163–165
  Baksa and, 19, 45
  biology curriculum changes and, 21, 33, 45, 70
  children of, 57
  Cleaver and, 14, 33
  creationism and, 16, 19–20, 23, 50, 59, 70, 207, 217
  deposition of, 73–77, 169–172
  description of, 11
  election to Dover school board, 10–11
  evolution theory rejection, 20–21
  First Amendment interpretation, 60
  Gillen and, 113
  intelligent design and, 30, 45, 59, 79, 218–219
  Kitzmiller trial and, 125, 168–172
  Kitzmiller verdict and, 198–199, 216–218
  misquote accusations of, 83–89
  Bryan Rehm and, 46
  religious beliefs, 11
  school board elections and, 91, 179
  on separation of church and state, 60
Bonsell, Brenda, 11, 219
Bonsell, Donald, 15, 90–91, 163, 170, 208, 209
Bonsell, Victoria, 57
Brennan, William J., 142, 196–197
Brown, Casey
  as Dover school board member, 15, 24, 33
  resignation from Dover school board, 46–47, 56
  Thomas More Law Center and, 29
Brown, Jeff
  as Dover school board member, 15, 23, 33
  intelligent design and, 29
  resignation from Dover school board, 47, 56, 180
  on Robertson, 180–181
  school tour, 11
  Thomas More Law Center and, 24
Brown University, 113–114
Bryan, William Jennings, 8, 38–39, 136–137
Buckingham, Bill

anonymous purchase of *Of Pandas and People*
    and, 163–165, 168–172, 208, 221
Baksa and, 33–34
biology curriculum debate and, 21, 23, 33,
    70
church attendance, 58
creationism, 15–16, 24, 29, 33–34, 50, 59,
    129, 207
deposition of, 77–78
Discovery Institute and, 37–38
intelligent design and, 30, 45, 59, 79
interview of prospective Dover Area School
    Board members, 56
Kitzmiller verdict and, 199, 222
marriage of, 101
misquote accusations of, 83–89
personal background, 14, 101–102
Pledge of Allegiance and, 21
prescription drug addiction of, 14–15, 31, 67,
    77, 102, 163, 174–175
resignation from school board, 94, 103, 177
on separation of church and state, 60
Spahr and, 46
surgery, 211, 220–221
testimony at *Kitzmiller* trial, 161–165
Thomas More Law Center and, 29
Thompson and, 59
Buckingham, Charlotte, 14, 24, 101
Buell, Jon, 139
Burdick Track, 182
Bush, George W.
    faith-based agendas, 16
    family values and, 36
    intelligent design support, 94–95
    Jones judicial appointment, 110–111, 214
    reelection of, 36, 59
Butler Act (Tennessee), 38

Callahan, Barrie
    biology textbook debate and, 22
    creationism and, 30
    as Dover school board member, 22
    Kitzmiller verdict and, 192–193, 196, 197, 198
    media and, 143
    patriotism of, 50
    Cyndi Sneath and, 174
    testimony at *Kitzmiller* trial, 126
Callahan, Fred, 6, 22, 50, 126–127, 143
Carville, James, 63
Cashman, James, 195
Center for Renewal of Science and Culture of
    Discovery Institute, 37, 43

chemistry, 19
Christ, 33–34, 89, 106, 107, 138
Cleaver, Jane, 13, 165
Cleese, John, 156
Cobb County case, 209
Colbert, Stephen, 213
Columbia Journalism Review, 97
Connecticut, 61
Cooper, Seth, 63
Creation Evidence Museum, 181
creationism curriculum. *See also* intelligent
    design
    Dover school board and, 15–16, 19–25, 29,
        33–34, 50, 59, 129, 140, 207, 217
    evolution theory balanced with, 23
    historical development of, 40
    as political platform, 11
    U.S. Supreme Court, 2, 33, 41, 139–141
Cumberland County Jail, 204–205

Daily Record, 161
Danbury Baptist Association, 61
Darrow, Clarence, 38
Darwin, Charles
    Pennsylvania Academic Standards and, 62
    photo in biology textbook, 16
    reluctance to publish, 184
    Robertson and, 180
    Scopes Monkey Trial and, 38
    Thompson and, 27, 211
    writings of, 62, 87, 99, 183, 199
Darwin, Emma, 184
Darwin on Trial (Johnson), 42
Darwinism, 23, 27, 38, 99, 137, 214
Darwin's Black Box (Behe), 117, 149, 154
Davis, Percival, 33
Dawkins, Richard, 42, 156
Dean, Cornelia, 95
Dembski, William, 43, 110, 138
Denton, Michael, 42
Descent of Man (Darwin), 87, 199
Descent of Man painting (Strausbaugh), 12
Design of Life, 210
Die Zeit, 157
Dinosaur Valley State Park, 181
Discovery Institute
    Center for Renewal of Science and Culture,
        37, 43
    evolution and, 37–38
    intelligent design and, 21, 43, 59, 98, 120
    Kitzmiller verdict and, 195–196
    news releases, 62

publications of, 156
purpose of, 97
staff attorneys, 120–121
Wedge Document, 44
DNA, 13, 21
Dobzhansky, Theodosius, 100
Domino's Pizza, 26
Dover Area School District. *See also Kitzmiller et al. v. Dover Area School District*; specific school board members
accusations of media misquotes and, 83–89, 166
biology textbook debate, 21–25, 33–36
creationism/evolution debate, 16, 19–25, 29, 140
Descent of Man painting and, 12–13
elections of school board, 91
intelligent design concept and, 28–30, 69, 140
intelligent design statement, 62, 80–81, 84–86, 122, 134
media and, 88
meeting procedures, 15
members of, 11, 14–16, 22
Pledge of Allegiance and, 21
population of, 9
school board elections, 177–179
school board presidents, 67
school prayer and, 13–14
superintendents and, 207–208
Thomas More Law Center and, 28–29, 66
Dover CARES, 91–93, 145–146, 177–180

Edwards v. Aguillard, 33, 35, 40–42, 139–141, 196–197
Elements of Journalism (Kovach and Rosenstiel), 96
Emig, Emily, 177
Emig, Terry, 177
Epperson, Susan, 39–40
Eshbach, Rob
evolutionary theory and, 16–19
father of, 25
"intelligent design statement" and, 81
as *Kitzmiller* plaintiff, 90–92
Kitzmiller verdict and, 195, 196
Spahr and, 174
Eshbach, Warren, 25, 180
Esquire, 131
Establishment Clause of First Amendment, 54, 193
Eveland, Beth, 58, 65, 92

Evolution: A Theory in Crisis (Denton), 42
evolution theory. *See also* creationism; intelligent design
challenges to prohibition of teaching of, 39–40
creationism balanced with, 23
evidence for, 16–17
faith and, 17
mechanics of, 3
overview of, 98
rejection of, 20–21
requirement for teaching, 62
revolution in evolution and, 59, 85–86
styles of teaching, 20

Fairie Fest, 119
faith-based agendas, 16
Falwell, Jerry, 36, 122
Fenimore, Deb, 58
First Amendment
creationism and, 23
Establishment Clause, 54, 193
evolution theory teaching and, 40
Free Exercise Clause, 54
"intelligent design statement" and, 122
Lebo and, 6
protection of reporter sources and, 121
Scopes Monkey Trial and, 38
separation of church and state and, 16, 60–61
flagellum, 116–117, 149–151
Flying Spaghetti Monster, 185–186
Forrest, Barbara, 137–143
fossil record, 19
Foundation for Thought and Ethics (FTE), 33, 138–139, 209–210
Fox News, 93, 162, 163, 203, 214
Frank, Thomas, 54
Franklin, Benjamin, 61
Free Exercise Clause of First Amendment, 54
Friendship United, 178

Galapagos, 28
Geesey, Heather, 125, 165–167, 177
Genesis Flood: The Biblical Record and Its Scientific Implications (Whitcomb and Morris), 26
genetic mutation, 99–100
Georgetown University, 184
Georgia, 209
Gilkyson, Eliza, 177
Gillen, Patrick, 71, 112–113, 124, 135, 168, 174–175

Gould, Steven Jay, 5, 98, 197
Gourds, 188
Great Tennessee Monkey Trial, 206
Grove, Jim, 119–120, 143–144, 206

Harkins, Sheila
  accusation against Maldonado, 88, 166
  Buckingham and, 221
  "intelligent design statement" and, 45
  at *Kitzmiller* trial, 125
  Nilsen and, 208
  on *Of Pandas and People*, 79
  school board elections and, 91, 179
  as school board president, 67, 71
Harmony Grove Community Church, 58,
  163
Harvard University, 98, 197
Harvey, Steve
  accommodations in Dover, 108
  Bonsell deposition and, 170
  depositions and, 71–73
  on Dover school board denial of use of
    creationism term, 82–83
  Kitzmiller trial proceedings and, 6, 161–165,
    168–172, 173
  media and, 65
  relationship with plaintiffs, 174
  Rothschild and, 55
Haught, John, 184–185
Henderson, Bobby, 186
Henson, Kate, 194
homosexuality, 90
Hovind, Kent, 65–66, 144
Human Genome Project, 13
Humburg, Burt, 144–145

Icons of Evolution (Wells), 21, 100
If Jesus Came Today, 206
Institute for Creation Research, 40, 113–114
intelligent design. *See also* creationism
  George W. Bush and, 94–95
  concept of, 59
  definitions of, 79, 98, 120, 136
  development of concept, 2, 41
  Dover school board and, 28–30, 69, 140
  DVDs about, 21–22
  media coverage of, 95–96
  school district statement, 62, 80–81, 84–86,
    122, 134
  supernatural and, 27, 112
  textbooks concerning, 27

*Intelligent Design: The Bridge Between Science
  and Theology* (Dembski), 138
Iraq, 13
Ivins, Molly, 108

Jefferson, Thomas, 61
Jesus Christ, 33–34, 89, 106, 107, 138
Johnson, Philip, 42–44, 210–211
Johnston, Dollar Bill, 189
Johnston, Max, 188–189
Jones, John E. III
  conferences in chambers of, 135
  criticism of, 214
  description of, 110, 212–213
  Geesey testimony and, 167–168
  hate mail and, 213
  humor expressed by, 176
  on judge's responsibility, 214–215
  Kitzmiller verdict, 192–196, 207, 222
  legislation concerning religion and, 71
  media and, 66, 212–213
  opinion of Rothschild cross-examination,
    153
  perjury investigation of Dover school board
    and, 199
  rulings during trial and, 118, 123, 141

Kanawha school board, 28
Kansas, 95, 209
Kansas Citizens for Science, 145
Kansas State Board of Education, 35–36, 186
Kansas State University, 144
Katskee, Richard, 55–56, 71–73, 140–141,
  174, 209
Kennedy, Donald, 95–96
Kennedy, John F., 64
Kenyon, Dean H., 21, 33, 139
Kerry, John, 59
Kevorkian, Jack, 26
Kitzmiller et al. v. Dover Area School District
  See also Dover Area School District; specific
    attorneys, plaintiffs, and defendants
  filing of, 64–65
  legal costs of, 207
  media coverage, 4–5, 63–65, 67, 111,
    115–116
  participants, 5–6
  verdict, 192–199
Kitzmiller, Jess, 50–51, 80–81, 84, 178, 195
Kitzmiller, Megan, 81, 178
Kitzmiller, Tammy
  children of, 50–51, 80–81

description of, 89
hate mail and, 213–214
Kitzmiller verdict and, 196, 197
outsider feelings of, 185
personal background, 51
school board elections and, 178
Cyndi Sneath and, 51, 52, 173
Knudsen, Paula, 52, 58
Kovach, Bill, 96
Ku Klux Klan, 87–88, 105

Lawson, James, 211–212
Lebo, Ann, 105
Lebo, Dean
ACLU and, 200
charitable work of, 204–205
death of, 205, 219–220
favorite scriptures, 222
frugality of, 203–204
grandchildren of, 223
Kitzmiller lawsuit and, 6–7, 129–130
as radio station owner, 3–4, 103–104
relationships with children, 190, 203
religious beliefs of, 4, 104–105, 130, 148
Lebo, Lynn, 107
Lehigh University, 116, 149
Leib, Joel, 58–59, 196
Lemon test, 122
Lemon v. Kurtzman, 71, 122
Liberty University, 122
Lippman, Walter, 96
Liquor Control Board (LCB), 110
Louisiana, 41
Luoni, John, 28
Luskin, Casey, 120–121
Lynn, Barry, 56
Lynn, Loretta, 1

Mabel, Sister, 146
Maldonado, Joe
accused of lying in reporting, 88, 166
as *Kitzmiller* trial witness, 121, 159–160
reporting on Dover school board meetings, 23–25, 30–32, 83
Marburger, John H., 94
Massachusetts, 177
Matzke, Nick, 35, 108, 131, 138–140, 173
May's Meeting House, 58
McLean v. Arkansas, 40–42
Mencken, H. L., 39, 116, 192, 199–200
Meyer, Stephen, 210
Michigan State University, 124

Miller, Jen, 16–18, 20, 81, 84, 215, 217
Miller, Judith, 121
Miller, Ken, 113–121, 194, 218
"Missing link," 19
Missouri School of Journalism, 159
Monaghan, Thomas, 26
Mooney, Chris, 97
moral relativism, 27, 211
Morris, Henry, 26, 40
Mt. Royal Assembly of God, 146
Muise, Robert, 27–28, 135, 149–150
mutation, 99–100
Myth of Separation (Barton), 60

Napierskie, David, 180
National Academy of Science, 151
National Center for Science Education
(NCSE), 35, 52–53, 63, 139, 197
natural selection, 17, 184, 217
Natural Theology, (Paley), 41
NBC, 193
Neiburg, Adele, 193
Nelson, Paul, 43
New York Times, 95, 121
New Yorker, 212
Nickol, Steve, 64
Nightline, 67
Nilsen, Richard
anonymous donation of *Of Pandas and People*
and, 44–45
creationism and, 20
description of, 72
Discovery Institute DVDs and, 21
evolution theory and, 16
Kitzmiller trial and, 71–73
ouster by school board, 207–208
Peterman and, 20
9/11 terrorist attacks, 9–10, 13
Nisbet, Matthew C., 97
Nixon, Richard, 64
North American Man/Boy Love Association,
177
North Salem Elementary, 32

O'Donnell, Liz, 193
Of Pandas and People (Davis and Kenyon)
anonymous purchase for Dover area schools,
44–45, 163–165, 168–172, 208, 221
creation defined in, 131
inaccuracies in, 112
"intelligent design statement" and, 62
Kitzmiller trial and, 79, 132–133, 138

Muise and, 150
proposed as Dover schools' biology text, 29, 33, 36
teacher criticism of, 82
West Virginia schools and, 27, 149
whales and, 132–133
O'Hair, Madalyn Murray, 213
Ohio, 34, 36, 63, 209
O'Reilly, Bill, 203, 214
Origin of Species (Darwin), 99, 183
Overton, William R., 40–41

Padian, Kevin, 131–134, 192
pagans, 119
Paine, Thomas, 48
Paley, William, 41, 112
Pandas. See Of Pandas and People
Parker, Randy, 158
Pell, Max, 23
Penn State University, 145
Penn, William, 58
Pennock, Robert, 124
Pennsylvania. *See also* Dover Area School District, 36–37, 52, 63–64, 175–176
Pennsylvania Academic Standards, 62
Pentecostal churches, 31–32, 93, 104, 146–148
Pepper Hamilton, 52, 55, 145, 166, 192, 194–196, 207
Peterman, Trudy, 20
physics, 20
Piltdown Man, 19
Plame, Valerie, 121
Platts, Todd, 14
Pledge of Allegiance, 14, 21, 72
prayer closets, 3–4
Priest, Karl, 27
"Project Steve Steve," 197

Racehorse Tavern, 48, 67–68, 173
radio
George W. Bush presidential election and, 59
Christian fundamentalism and, 3–4
Lebo's conversion story and, 103–104
9/11 terrorist attacks and, 10
Raulston, John T., 38–39
Ray, Larry, 204
Reagan, Ronald, 42
Reeser, Larry, 10–13
Rehm, Alix, 57–58
Rehm, Bryan
at ACLU conference, 212
Bonsell and, 46

Buckingham and, 56
creationism curriculum and, 20, 24
description of, 57
intelligent design DVDs and, 22
media and, 63, 65
personal background, 6, 56–57
Racehorse Tavern meetings and, 173
school board elections and, 91–92, 146, 177
as school board member, 208–209
on science in Dover schools, 215–216
videotaping school board meetings, 66
Rehm, Christy
at ACLU conference, 212
description of, 57
Halloween costume, 116
Kitzmiller verdict and, 194–195, 196
personal background, 6, 57
relationship with husband, 20
school board elections and, 146
testimony at *Kitzmiller* trial, 125–126
Reinking, Bernie, 92, 179
Republican National Committee, 61
"Response to Critics of *Darwin's Black Box*" (Behe), 156
Rhode Island, 37
Riddle, Eric, 178
Ridge, Tom, 110–111
Robertson, Pat, 180–181
Rolling Stone, 143
Rosenstiel, Tom, 96
Rothschild, Allison, 5
Rothschild, Eric
at ACLU conference, 212
bacteria flagellum and, 116
Big Bang theory and, 136
Cobb County case and, 209
depositions and, 71–77
filing of *Kitzmiller* and, 65
injunction against reading "intelligent design statement," 80–81
jogging route, 108–109
Kitzmiller trial proceedings and, 112, 118, 127, 138, 151–157, 175–176, 210
Kitzmiller verdict and, 194, 196
media and, 5
National Center for Science Education and, 52–53
physical description of, 152–153
relationship with plaintiffs, 174
Scott and, 52–54
Rothschild, Walter, 152–153
Rowand, Ed

Buckingham and, 221
as Dover school board member, 93–94
at *Kitzmiller* trial, 125, 142–143
personal background, 93–94
Christy Rehm and, 146
relationship with father, 172
Russell, Steve, 34
Russia, 40

Sam & Tony's, 15
Sanders, Larry J., 119
Santorum, Rick, 110
Schlafly, Phyllis, 214
Schmidt, Tom, 55, 166, 174
school prayer
    Cleaver and, 13, 165
    Dover Area School District, 13–14
    as political platform, 11
Science, 95
science, definitions of, 40–41, 186
scientific theory defined, 151
Scopes, John, 38
Scopes Monkey Trial, 8, 38–39, 180,
    199–200, 206
Scott, Eugenie, 35, 52–54, 192, 197
Second-Chance Ministries, 204
separation of church and state, 60–61
700 Club, 180
Sherlock, Jenn, 84, 163
Short, Ron, 177
Smith, Julie, 58, 93, 135–136
Smith, Katherine, 58
Smith, Will, 213
Sneath, Cyndi
    ACLU and, 52, 212
    Barrie Callahan and, 174
    children of, 51
    Tammy Kitzmiller and, 51, 52, 173
    Kitzmiller verdict and, 193–195
    media and, 65, 143
    personal background, 6
    school board elections and, 91–92, 178–179
    as witness at *Kitzmiller* trial, 126, 127–129
Sneath, Griffin, 6, 51
Sneath, Nate, 51
Sneath, Paul, 52
social Darwinism, 38, 137
Solidarity Movement, 201
Son Volt, 189
Southeastern Louisiana University, 137
Spahr, Bertha
    creationism and, 24

effect of lawsuit on, 66, 192
Eshbach and, 174
Kitzmiller verdict and, 195
Of Pandas and People and, 45
personal background, 19
refusal to read "intelligent design statement,"
    81–82
religion in schools and, 46
students and, 18–19
Springsteen, Bruce, 131
Sputnik, 40
Starr, Michelle, 161, 198
Stough, Ashley, 49
Stough, Steve
    ACLU and, 50, 211–212
    Dover school board meetings and, 6
    intelligent design and, 51
    Kitzmiller verdict and, 192–194
    personal background, 48–50
    plaintiff meetings and, 67–68
    response to Thompson, 136
    response to verdict, 5–6
    school board elections and, 91, 178–179
Stough, Susan, 66
Strausbaugh, Zach, 12, 19

Talbot, Margaret, 212–213
tattoos, 186–187
"Tear Stained Eye" (Son Volt), 189
Tennessee, 38–39, 105
Texas, 181–189
Thomas More Law Center *See also* specific
    attorneys
    advisory board, 110
    depositions and, 71
    Dover Area School District and, 28–29, 66
    intelligent design quest of, 28–29, 34, 36
    mission statement, 27
    overview of, 26
    teacher refusal to read "intelligent design
        statement" and, 82
Thompson, Richard
    description of, 135
    injunction against reading "intelligent design
        statement" and, 69
    intelligent design definition and, 136
    Kevorkian and, 26
    Kitzmiller verdict and, 197–198
    media and, 135
    moral relativism and, 27, 211
    revolution in evolution and, 59, 85–86
    trial strategy, 102–103, 126, 141

Three Mile Island, 53
Time magazine, 213
tolerance, 10
Touchstone, 44
Treaty of Tripoli, 61
Tripoli Treaty, 61

Uncommon Descent (Dembski), 110–111
University of California, Berkeley, 43, 132
Unlocking the Mystery of Life (Kenyon), 21
U.S. Constitution. *See* First Amendment
U.S. Supreme Court *See also Edwards v.*
    Aguillard; Lemon v. Kurtzman
  creation science and, 2, 33, 41, 139–141
  evolution theory teaching and, 39–40
  Lemon test, 122
  Pledge of Allegiance and, 21

Virginia, 189

Walczak, Kathy, 201
Walczak, Witold "Vic"
  accommodations in Dover, 108
  depositions and, 71
  journalist protection of sources and, 122–123
  Kitzmiller trial proceedings and, 114–115,
    118–119, 131, 132, 151, 156, 159–160
  Kitzmiller verdict and, 194, 196
  marriage of, 201
  as outsider, 55
  Pennsylvania legal director of ACLU, 54

personal background, 200–203
relationship with plaintiffs, 174
restraining orders and, 80
Scott and, 54
Walesa, Lech, 201
Wallace, Alfred Russel, 184
Wedge Document, 44
Wells, Jonathan, 21, 43, 100–101
Wenrich, Noel, 11, 23, 47
West Virginia, 27–28, 149
whales, 132–133
What's the Matter with Kansas (Frank), 54
Whitcomb, John, 26
White, Ed, 123, 160
Why Evolution Is Stupid (Hovind), 144
Williams, Walter, 159
Wise, Kurt, 43

Yingling, Angie, 33
York County Homeschool Association, 89
York Daily Record
  accusations of misreporting and, 83–89
  editorial on biology textbook controversy, 45
  Kitmiller trial reportage, 157
  letters to editor, 167
  reporters for, 2, 23, 30, 115
York Dispatch, 23, 76, 161
Yorktowne Hotel, 15
Young, Charlie, 223
Young, Lesli, 223
Young, Maxwell Dean, 223–224